TRANSFORMATION

TRANSFORMATION

*Creating an Exceptional Life in
the Face of Cancer*

By Gale M. O'Brien

Transformation: Creating an Exceptional Life in the Face of Cancer

Published by Gale M. O'Brien

P.O. Box 20713

Albuquerque, NM 87154

Copyright © 2013 Gale M. O'Brien

All rights reserved. No part of this publication may be reproduced or utilized without the written permission from the publisher, except as acknowledged quotes presented in literary articles, reviews or research.

Cover and interior design by CreateSpace, an Amazon.com Company

Logo design by Hilary Klein

Principal photography by Gale M. O'Brien

Note: The information in this book is for educational purposes only and is not recommended as a means of diagnosing or treating an illness. All matters concerning physical and mental health should be supervised by a health practitioner knowledgeable in treating that particular condition. Neither the publisher nor author directly or indirectly dispense medical advice or assume any responsibility for those who choose to treat themselves.

ISBN 10: **1492923990**

ISBN 13: **978-1492923992**

DEDICATION

To my sons, Wes and Brad,

I will love you always.

FOREWORD

The American Cancer Society estimates that about 1,660,290 new cancer cases will be diagnosed in 2013. Because you are reading this affirms that you or someone you care for has recently been diagnosed with cancer. Even though this is a very lonely place, I can assure you that you are not alone. Living with cancer involves much more than being able to identify the stage of the cancer or the best treatment options. This book provides a plan for those who journey this unfamiliar territory. You will learn not only how to survive following diagnosis and treatment, but also how to flourish and become a better you!

Gale O'Brien and I met about five years ago at church. This beautiful, self-confident, personable, and cheerful woman

TRANSFORMATION

graciously invited me into her circle of friends. Then the unimaginable happened. Gale was diagnosed with breast cancer and I watched her unravel, physically and emotionally. As a mammography technologist, educator on breast disease, and a breast cancer survivor myself, Gale's response was all too familiar to me. The roller coaster of emotions is something that all women have in common at the time of diagnosis.

Gale used her exceptional organizational skills to develop a plan-of-attack. She aggressively transformed her negative thinking and intentionally sought alternative methods of action. This book is a pathway to healing for all cancer patients. My only regret is that this exceptional resource was not available fifteen years ago when I was diagnosed with breast cancer. Instead, I stumbled through the extended healing process feeling hopeless and alone.

Each of us can profoundly change our own life as documented by Gale's actions. By carefully planning your time, seeking rewarding friendships, developing trust in your medical team, and connecting with your spiritual self, the cancer patient learns

FOREWORD

that the journey is not his or her own. Rather, the journey includes countless others who have come before you. A cancer survivor's experiences and shared feelings are credible and highly valued because they offer hope to those who struggle. By sharing the contents of this book, the reader can personally help others diagnosed with cancer. Peace.

Jeanette R. Joyce

Founder & Educational Director, RadComm, Inc.

Mammography Technologist,

Breast Cancer Survivor

ACKNOWLEDGMENTS

Writing a book is not an easy process. It requires dedication, commitment, encouragement and resources. As a first time author, this book was possible with the collaborative efforts of my medical team, my family, my friends, my life coaches, Janis Pullen and Barbara Lemaire, and the many cancer patients and survivors who shared their journey with me. I thank you all from the bottom of my heart.

To my breast surgeon, Dr. Linda Ann Smith, who did an excellent job of preserving as much tissue and making me look symmetrical. To my medical oncologist, Dr. Lovie Bey, for her kind and intuitive bedside manner. To Dr. Steven Gough who calmed my fears and patiently answered all of my questions when

TRANSFORMATION

I was facing prophylactic surgery. To my acupuncturist, Dr. Ann Losee, who restored my well being when I had wasted away with nausea, depression and bone pain. To my physical therapists, Ada Portman and Melu Uriarte, whose tender touch and cavalry of exercises allowed me to regain full range of motion in both of my arms.

To my dear friend, Jeanette Joyce, who spent countless hours with me while I was going through cancer treatments. Jeanette is a rare friend and colleague whose generosity and listening ear can't be match. She prepared weekly meals and made herself available to me at any time of day or night. Thank you for your friendship Jeanette.

To my Sunday Sistas, Karen, Michelle, Judy, Marita, Gaylene, Rudi and Patti whose loyal friendship and monthly get-togethers sustain me with laughter and fun in both good times and hard times.

To my family for their unwavering love and support. Thank you for making multiple trips to be with me during my surgeries

ACKNOWLEDGMENTS

and cancer treatments. I'm forever grateful to you for being there for me and relieving the loneliness that so often comes with a cancer diagnosis.

To my son and news reporter, Wes Duplantier, for his weekly edits of each chapter of my book. Your feedback was invaluable.

To the authors who inspired me throughout this process. I am forever a fan: Arianna Huffington, Stephen King, Marianne Williamson, Susan M. Love, M.D., Bernie Siegel, M.D., Wendy Schlessel Harpham, M.D., David Servan-Schreiber, M.D., Ph.D., and Nancy Jill Thames.

- Gale O'Brien

PREFACE

This book is my experience through cancer, how I survived it and created a full life afterwards. It's both autobiographical and educational. It's an honest, revealing and no holds barred description of my transformational journey to survival. I want to emphasize the word "survival" because that is the life I have lived all along. My life has been a series of lessons learned, reinvention and survival. I have three college degrees and three teaching credentials. I may look intelligent on paper but my real smarts came from living life - from falling down and picking myself up. I often find myself asking the question, "How did I get here?" In other words, "How did I get myself into this awful mess?" Like the time I thought there was enough clearance under

TRANSFORMATION

my car to drive *over* a diesel tire laying in the middle of the road. Or like the time I drove my car 50 mph, with the cruise control *on*, down a snowy mountain highway. Both situations proved to be disastrous, but I did learn important lessons and I came out alive! No college course taught me how to beat cancer. I've survived cancer because of my unsinkable determination and my thirst for living life.

I was given many books to read at the beginning of my diagnosis. They were interesting but none of them actually explained in detail what cancer would feel like, look like, or be like as it was happening to you. My motivation for writing this book began as outlet for my emotions, feelings and thoughts as I was experiencing cancer. In the period of one year, October to September, my whole body went through a metamorphous that could only be documented through words and photographs. The process of watching my body change was both scary and fascinating. Even more intriguing, was how my mind and my thinking changed on so many topics. I wrote this

PREFACE

book to encourage patients, survivors, caregivers and anyone encountering a serious illness to view disease as a phase to pass through with the hope of knowing that an exceptional life is waiting ahead.

CONTENTS

Foreword vii

Acknowledgments xi

Preface xv

Introduction xxiii

Chapter 1: My Story 1

    My Life Before Cancer 1

    Turning 50 4

    Cancer Diagnosis 5

    Stages of Grief 8

Chapter 2: Cancer Treatments 11

    Chemotherapy 12

    Setting an Intention to Live 14

    Radiation therapy 16

Physical therapy 21

Prophylactic surgery 22

Chapter 3: Food **25**

Feeding your body exceptional food 26

Super-foods 28

Juicing and Blending 31

Understanding the role of sugar 36

Building back the immune system 64

Chapter 4: Health & Fitness **67**

How to find exceptional healthcare 67

Western vs. Eastern medicine 69

Cancer: A Complementary Approach by Dr. Ann Losee . . 71

Why fitness is important to an exceptional life 77

Chapter 5: Beauty **81**

Beauty and cancer 81

What defines beauty? by Shannon Hoskovec 84

Hair care 87

Organic beauty products by Nicole Kuhlmann 89

CONTENTS

Chapter 6: Attitude & Passion **93**

    Changing perceptions and attitude 93

    A Positive ALTITUDE by Martha Powell 95

    What's your passion? 97

    Pay It Forward by Gayle Allen 100

    Developing your bucket list 101

Chapter 7: Time **109**

    Perfectionism 110

    Control 111

    Busyness 113

    People 114

Chapter 8: Relationships **117**

    Getting healthy in relationships 118

    Letting go of emotional repression 120

    Experiencing joy in relationships 123

    How to stay connected to others 125

    Social Media, Blogs, & the Internet by Barbara

    Lemaire, PhD. 126

TRANSFORMATION

Chapter 9: Fear **129**
   Of death and dying 130
   Of cancer reoccurrence 133
   Of living life exceptionally well 135

Chapter 10: Spirituality **139**
   My spiritual journey 139
   Daily affirmations and devotions 141
   The spiritual side of an exceptional life 144
   Perseverance by Jo Anne Parish 145
   Foundations for spiritual living 150

Conclusion **153**
   Survivorship 155
   Creating your own exceptional life 156

Appendix I: 10 Tips to Feel Exceptional During Cancer
              Treatment 159

Appendix II: Resource Guide 165

Notes 175

INTRODUCTION

Perseverance, determination, drive, resolve, courage and grit. These are the characteristics of a true survivor. A cancer survivor has to look death in the face. She either gets scared and her body succumbs or she sets an intention to live and beats the cancer against all odds. This book is about the latter. It's about taking the reins of your life and proactively changing the course of your survival, from diagnosis to treatment to creating a new life after cancer.

When I was first diagnosed with cancer, I struggled with having a purpose. I was unable to work full time while I was in treatment because of the frequency of medical appointments, the physical therapy and the debilitating side effects. At times, I felt useless and unproductive. I wondered to myself, "Am I needed anymore?" "If so, then what is my purpose now?" For the first time, I realized that life was finite. I also realized that my remaining time on earth was limited by the status of my health and my survival. It suddenly became clear that my purpose as a cancer patient was to work at keeping my body in optimal health so that I could receive my chemotherapy and daily radiation therapy on schedule. My job as a cancer survivor is to keep a healthy immune system, to feed my body the best foods available, to be physically fit and to stay informed on advances in cancer research and treatments to insure my survival will lead to a long life.

After discovering my purpose, I became overwhelmed with the feeling of wanting to live my life fully and exceptionally. I began to work with a life coach to help me look outside the normal context of life and to create an openness toward what could lie ahead in my life after cancer. For the first time, I realized that I could fashion a life that was enjoyable, if not extraordinary. My new life after cancer could become an exceptional life to live.

INTRODUCTION

Exceptional is to be an exception; to be uncommon; to be well above average; to be extraordinary. So what had been holding me back from living an exceptional life until now? Family, friends, money, time or was it fear? Marianne Williamson writes in her book, *A Return to Love* that, "Our deepest fear is not that we are inadequate. Our deepest fear is that we are powerful beyond measure. It is our light, not our darkness, that most frightens us. We ask ourselves, who am I to be brilliant, gorgeous, talented, fabulous? Actually, who are you not to be? You are a child of God. Your playing small doesn't serve the world. There's nothing enlightened about shrinking so that other people won't feel insecure around you. We are all meant to shine, as children do. We were born to make manifest the glory of God that is within us. It's not just in some of us; it's in everyone. And as we let our own light shine, we unconsciously give other people permission to do the same. As we're liberated from our own fear, our presence automatically liberates others."[1]

This book explores the passion for living that lies inside of each us. Take a moment to ask yourself, "What truly excites me in life?" Is it people, food, travel, work, sports or the arts? Do you have a bucket list of things you want to do before you die? Now is the time to move those must-do items to your real life plan. Your exceptional life plan! In order for your exceptional life to be complete, you'll need to consider your health and fitness. Why is fitness important to an exceptional life? I'll also discuss what exceptional food is and how you can create exceptional health by becoming an active member of your medical team. Finally, I'll explore the spiritual side of an exceptional life. How can you use the gifts of spirituality to enhance your life? If you've ever wondered can I really have it all, the answer is "Yes, you can." An exceptional life is a balanced life filled with pursuits that you truly *want* to do.

CHAPTER 1
MY STORY

"When you stand and share your story in an empowering way, your story will heal you and your story will heal somebody else."

~Iyanla Vanzant

MY LIFE BEFORE CANCER

It's important for me to share with you my life before cancer because I believe that each of us is the sum of all our life experiences. I was born in Philadelphia, Pennsylvania in 1961. However, I was raised along with my three sisters in Silicon Valley, California from the age of one until I went away to college. For the most part, my childhood was normal and I benefited greatly from having a stay-at-home mother and a father who was a good provider. Perhaps, what stands out the most as I reflect back on my childhood is an abundance of sunshine and the inability to express my feelings. I clearly remember feeling stifled, confused, and mostly shy about sharing my voice because it was more important to be respectful and well behaved.

Aside from the sunshine and my repressed emotions, I learned three important lessons in my childhood. Wear shoes when riding a bicycle. Don't run through the house, especially when approaching a sliding glass door. Finally, look straight ahead when walking down a busy sidewalk. Why were these significant lessons? For starters, I almost lost a toe riding my bicycle barefoot. Secondly, I ended up with a large goose egg bump on my forehead from walking into a stop sign while talking to my friends. Finally, what I learned the most from these experiences was to pay attention to what I'm doing because life has consequences.

Sunshine followed me to college as I attended California Polytechnic State University in San Luis Obispo, California where I met my first husband. After college graduation, he was commissioned as an officer in the U.S. Army and we were stationed in Oahu, Hawaii. This was a happy time of our marriage as we spent almost every weekend at the beach on the North Shore or visiting the other islands. When his tour of duty ended after four years, we returned to Silicon Valley to find employment and later moved to the Central Valley of California to raise our two sons. Our marriage was challenged on many levels when both of our children were diagnosed with serious illnesses in infancy and as toddlers. In the second half of this marriage, I remember my emotional repression reaching a peak and it was at this time that my first marriage collapsed.

While I was going through my protracted divorce, my mother was undergoing cancer treatment for lymphoma. She bravely fought her battle for 10 years, but sadly she passed away exactly one month before my wedding to my second husband. In retrospect, I realize now that I never allowed myself to fully grieve her passing because I was so caught up in wedding planning and becoming a new stepparent to three more children. Again, more bottled up emotions were swept under the carpet.

TRANSFORMATION

In 2006, I moved with my second husband to New Mexico to support his corporate career. Again, I found myself living in a state with predominately sunny weather and hot temperatures. Over the course of 46 years, living in California, Hawaii and New Mexico, I was diagnosed with skin cancer three times. I was fortunate each time that my diagnosis was basil cell carcinoma, the least deadliest form of skin cancer. After each surgery, I took precautions to protect my skin from the harmful ultraviolet rays of the sun by wearing an assortment of hats, sunglasses and sunscreen. Although I had a history of skin cancer, I never dwelled on it or felt threatened that my life was in jeopardy.

TURNING 50

Like most people approaching middle age, my fiftieth birthday was a significant milestone but emotionally it felt like a bomb had exploded. During this year, I had resigned from my teaching career, my last child went off to college, my second marriage ended, and I made a cross-country move by myself. For most of my life, I had used emotional repression as a coping mechanism to deal with the most traumatic events in my life. There had been so much chaos that had transpired in my adult life, that I simply had to find a way to put my game face on and charge forward. Little did I know the toll all of this was taking on my health.

CANCER DIAGNOSIS

In October 2012, I was diagnosed with stage two breast cancer. I received a phone call from the breast imaging center two days before my father's wedding. The news of a cancer diagnosis never arrives at a good time, so I chose to keep it private until after the wedding. When I returned home, I brought a friend with me to my initial appointment with the breast surgeon because I was afraid that I might fall apart in tears and not be able to listen and take notes.

After the initial biopsy revealed breast cancer, I was quickly scheduled for two breast MRIs, a full body CAT scan, a colonoscopy, a pelvic ultrasound and a multiple gate acquisition scan of my heart. I was so overwhelmed with medical procedures that I don't think I came up for air for close to six weeks after my first biopsy.

TRANSFORMATION

My father and my stepmother flew out to be with me during my surgery. I had a lumpectomy and a sentinel lymph node biopsy. When I awoke in the recovery room, the nurse explained to me that I had a drainage tube sewn into my chest wall to drain the fluids out my incision site. She also told me that my health insurance would not cover for a home healthcare professional to assist me with the drain so therefore my parents would need to be trained on drain care. My Dad and I both looked at each in shock. Fortunately, my stepmother had been a registered nurse and she knew exactly what to do with the drain. I understood the necessity of the drain, but I found it uncomfortable and disgusting and couldn't wait for it to be removed. Five days later, I went to the breast surgeon's office to have my sutures removed and the nurse just yanked the drain out of me on the count of three. When I asked about stitches to close up the hole, I was told that it would heal on its own.

On November 26, 2012, I met with my oncologist to discuss my treatment plan. My pathology work revealed that I had two types of breast cancer. The first one was ductal carcinoma in situ which was small and contained. The second cancer was an aggressive and invasive ductal cancer that had spread to one of the five lymph nodes that were removed during my surgery. My cancer was estrogen and progesterone receptor positive. My oncologist explained that my treatment would involve eight rounds of chemotherapy, six weeks of radiation therapy and five to ten years of Tamoxifen, an oral drug which acts as a hormone inhibitor. The good news was that my CAT scan, colonoscopy, pelvic ultrasound all came back free of cancer.

Next, I was scheduled for a surgery to insert a port-a-catheter into my neck so that I could receive my chemotherapy drugs without having to have an I.V. put into my arm each time. I really didn't want a port-a-catheter. The thought of something foreign implanted into my neck and chest sounded awful. I was nervous about the procedure and asked a friend who had gone through the surgery before to join me. On the day of the surgery, the nurse gave me a drug in my arm that only relaxed me but did not put me to sleep. I was awake during the entire surgery! I didn't feel any pain, but I could hear everything the doctors were saying during the procedure. Afterwards, I had two incisions, one in my chest and one in my neck. I experienced considerable pain and pressure on my right side for up to a week. Three days later, I was at the oncology clinic receiving my first chemotherapy infusion.

STAGES OF GRIEF

In 1969, Elisabeth Kubler-Ross' book, *On Death and Dying*, proposed the now famous Five Stages of Grief as a pattern of adjustment. These five stages of grief are denial, anger, bargaining, depression, and acceptance. She wrote, "In general, individuals experience most of these stages, though in no defined sequence, after being faced with the reality of their impending death."[2]

I've experienced the stages of grief on a few occasions in my life; when I went through my divorces and now with a diagnosis of breast cancer. During the first week of my diagnosis, I was in denial. Every time the doctor's office called to schedule me for another diagnostic MRI, EKG, or CAT scan, I would ask, "Are you *sure* you have the right patient? My name is Gale O'Brien." To my astonishment, each time I'd ask, the medical assistant would confirm my name, my birthdate and my diagnosis.

For me, the two stages I seem to get stuck on are anger and depression. My anger would begin by me asking God, "Why me? Haven't I gone through enough trauma and tragedy in my life?" I can remember sobbing at night and screaming out, "I don't want cancer! "I don't want chemotherapy!" "I don't want radiation!" I wanted so badly to pack my suitcases and move back home with my Dad and my sisters. Never had I been so scared in my life to go through something so big alone by myself. I can remember trembling and shaking when I cry because I was so scared that the chemotherapy drugs were going to kill me while I was sleeping. When I'd awake the next morning, I was always surprised to still be alive.

Once I began chemotherapy, however, my anger immediately switch to hatred, specifically hatred toward food. My tastebuds seemed to change overnight. Almost all food tasted like cardboard and every drink, including water, tasted like dish soap. It began by me hating some foods, then most foods, then all foods. I could not

TRANSFORMATION

construct a grocery list, open a refrigerator, go into a grocery store or even cook a meal without feeling completely nauseated. I lost 25 pounds and then my hatred shifted to people. I began to hate some people, then most people. I mostly hated people who didn't have cancer. In my crazy, nauseated head, I believed they didn't truly understand what a nightmare cancer was. I would secretly pray at night that they would be diagnosed with a terminal disease and die a painful death. It appeared that I was in a vicious cycle that I couldn't break free from. Before my hatred grew to hating all people, I decided to seek professional health. I began twice weekly treatments with an acupuncturist. After two weeks, my nausea began to subside and my anger and hatred also settled into a more manageable place. I had to stay diligent and committed to going regularly until the end of my chemotherapy.

CHAPTER 2
CANCER TREATMENTS

"We have two options, medically and emotionally:

give up or fight like hell."

~ Lance Armstrong

I made up my mind early on in my diagnosis that I would seek out the best treatment available to combat my cancer. My number one goal was to live a long and fruitful life. I also felt a responsibility to my children, my family and my friends to fight the good fight and to give it my all. I agreed to all recommended surgeries and lifesaving treatments in a profound effort to live. The remaining odds in my survival are now in God's hands.

CHEMOTHERAPY

During my chemotherapy treatment, I was racked with fear and anxiety that would begin on Day 1 of my chemo cycle and usually last through Day 5. Then I would begin to feel better physically, my mental disposition would improve and I would start to feel confident about myself again and hopeful for my future.

These feelings of anxiety would come on me while I was isolated in my house due to my white blood cell count being low and having to stay out of public places. I learned a lot about myself during the first five days of each chemo cycle. I learned that I don't like to be alone. I need to socialize and be surrounded by friends and family. I also felt my worst physically ~ nauseous, tired, sore with bone pain, malaise, depression, and a general disinterest in everything (food, people, chores, life, everything). My physical pain made me angry at cancer. I hated being sick with cancer. I hated not being able to work outside the home. I hated not having hair, discolored finger nails, no eye brows, no eye lashes. It was very hard to like myself because every morning I saw an alien in the bathroom mirror staring back at me.

CANCER TREATMENTS

After my third chemo infusion, I developed terrible neuropathy in my hands. Neuropathy usually starts in the hands and/or feet and creeps up the arms and legs. Sometimes it feels like tingling or numbness. Other times, it's more of a shooting or burning pain or sensitivity to temperature. My neuropathy began to interfere with normal day-to-day function such as zipping a zipper, twisting the cap off a water bottle, writing legibly with a pen. My red, painful hands made me feel sad and more depressed. When I arrived for my fourth infusion, not only did I have neuropathy in my hands, but I was seriously dizzy every time I stood up from sitting down.

My oncologist performed some tests on me and determined that I was severely dehydrated. She halted my chemo infusion and instead I received three bags of fluids into my port and was given an assignment to drink 70 ounces of fluid a day until the end of my chemotherapy treatments. Immediately, I began to feel better. For the first time since I began chemo, I experienced what it was like to have a bowel movement with a colon that was hydrated

- no more constipation! My dizziness went away. I was now mentally alert and could make intelligent decisions. After about three days of faithfully drinking my fluids, the neuropathy in my hands began to go away. It was truly a miracle as I had no idea that my neuropathy was caused from being dehydrated.

SETTING AN INTENTION TO LIVE

When I was first diagnosed with cancer, I was very frightened about my prognosis and whether I'd survive. Previously, I had watched friends and family go through cancer treatments and found it very upsetting and scary. Given my fear, I decided to be an obedient patient and do everything my doctors told me to do. I thought by being submissive that my survival rate would increase and my fears would go away. In theory, I was operating with negative energy toward my cancer diagnosis.

Interestingly, after I had completed all required diagnostic testing before starting chemotherapy, I found that I was still scared. Now, I was afraid that the chemotherapy drugs would weaken me and eventually kill me. I had been told by the oncology

CANCER TREATMENTS

nurses that chemotherapy weakens the body and therefore I could expect to 'feel bad.' I was so fearful about my first infusion, that I rushed to address and mail all my Christmas cards by the first week of December just in case I didn't survive the first round! I continue this negative energy through my first three chemo infusions.

Then something magical happened. A friend, who is a 18 year cancer survivor, accompanied me to my fourth infusion. On the thirty minute drive to the oncology clinic, I expressed my fears and asked her what her secret was for surviving cancer so long. She told me about a book she had read during her cancer treatments titled *Love, Medicine, & Miracles* by Bernie Siegel, MD. My friend explained that setting an intention to survive cancer could have a positive affect on my healing process. So when I returned home, I began to research Dr. Siegel's philosophy.

I discovered that through his work as a surgeon and founder of the Exceptional Cancer Patients therapy group, Dr. Siegel had learned that cancer patients who developed a healthy self-love and gave up their emotional repression were able to improve their immune system, overcome cancer and improve their survival rate. He also wrote about individuals with a high *inner locus of control* who believe that events in their life were derived primarily from their own actions. In other words, patients who took control of their health and became active members of their medical team were shown to live longer.[3]

It was then that I set an intention to live and starting operating with positive energy toward my cancer. I chose to receive twice weekly acupuncture treatments for my nausea, depression and bone pain. I also chose to start exercising twice a week using the treadmill and weight lighting to build up my endurance and to improve both my physical and mental health. After my fifth chemo infusion, I knew I was on the home stretch with only three more chemo cycles to go. I no longer felt sad, vulnerable, helpless, nor fatal. I felt whole again. I was determined to live!

RADIATION THERAPY

I had been told by friends that radiation therapy was "a piece of cake." Doctors and nurses reassured me that if I survive chemotherapy, then radiation would be "a walk in the park." I found the experience to be frightening and painful. I was not alone in my thoughts. Many of the patients who had the same appointment time as I did at the cancer center expressed their worries to me about their treatment. I talked with patients who were going through pancreatic cancer, prostate cancer, throat cancer, and breast cancer. Everybody seemed to be feeling their way through the experience. One man with throat cancer had his neck so burned from radiation that he'd lost the entire first layer of skin. He looked over at me one day with his toothless smile and said, "Just smoke a little marijuana each day and you'll be able get through this." I hesitated and thought maybe I'd feel differently if my cancer was diagnosed at Stage 4.

During the initial consultation with the radiation oncologist, the doctor informed me of the most common reactions to radiation - skin changes, redness, irritation, possible blistering and extreme fatigue. What you don't know until you get home and read through the disclosure and consent for radiation oncology are the late reactions - stiffness and discomfort in the shoulder joint, rib or lung damage causing pain, fracture, cough, shortness of breath, nerve damage causing pain or loss of feeling in the arm, damage to the heart muscle or sac leading to heart failure, and that secondary cancers may develop in or adjacent to the irradiated area. Reading all of this was enough to make me want to call the oncologist and cancel my whole course of treatment! I didn't.

I nervously kept my appointment for simulation which was a treatment planning session. During this appointment, a CT scan and X-rays were taken to create a three dimensional picture of my treatment area. In addition, the radiation technician created a customized mold of my upper torso, called a cradle, that I laid in for each of my treatments. Most surprising of all were the marks that were drawn on my body and secured by covering them with tape. When I was excused to the dressing room to change back into my street clothes, I was shocked to discover red Sharpie pen marks drawn up and out of my neck line. How was I supposed to conduct business in public or even begin to explain the pen marks to others?

CANCER TREATMENTS

Despite everything involved, I remained committed to completing my radiation therapy. Half way through my treatment, I went through a second planning session. This time it was for the "boost" of radiation I would receive directly to my incision during the last five days of treatment. I had to lie on my side with my left arm over my head. With my breast all exposed, a male radiation technician used a compression device to smash my breast flat so my incision could be marked with Sharpie pens. While trapped under this compression device, I was pushed into the CT scan machine for another round of X-rays. Once again, I found myself having a conversation with God. "How did I get here?" "Why do I have cancer?" "I HATE this!"

During my radiation therapy, I experienced an ominous feeling every time I laid in my cradle and that giant round machine came over my head and positioned itself directly in front of my heart. Huge infrared lights drew the outline of my treatment area onto my chest. Finally, there was the sound of the radiation doses catapulting out of the mother machine like an ancient military device. It was then that I sent up a prayer to God asking him to lay a hand on the technicians who were guiding the radiation beam into my body and another hand on my shoulder to keep me safe to the end of my therapy.

At the beginning of my fourth week of radiation, the left side of my chest and underarm started turning red like a sunburn. However, during my fifth week, the redness turned into burns with extreme charring under my left armpit. I found some relief by putting a frozen bag of peas on it several times a day. However, the pain was so severe that Tylenol and Motrin barely touched it. Every Tuesday while I was in treatment, I was seen by my radiation oncologist. He would inspect my treatment area to access my progress through radiation. When I asked him for a prescription for pain medication, such as Vicodin, he told me it wasn't necessary and that perhaps I needed a referral to see a psychiatrist. I was totally surprised by his response. A psychiatrist? Are you kidding me? I wanted to ask him, "Have you ever had your chest wall radiated to the point of second degree burns!" I was speechless.

He just patted me on the shoulder and again offered to write a referral for psychiatrist. I eventually got the Vicodin, but this was after complaining to the social worker at the cancer center.

PHYSICAL THERAPY

I began receiving physical therapy for the first time about a month after my lumpectomy. I noticed weakness in my left arm while trying to pull a door open and while carrying bags of groceries. The feeling was hard to describe at first. It felt like an overall soreness, followed by tingling that interfered with daily functioning. I was fitted with a compression sleeve which helped tremendously. I was also given at home exercises for my pectoral muscles, shoulder joint and arm muscles. The physical therapist also used a tool to "comb" my incision. This somewhat painful procedure was necessary to prevent my incision from becoming a ropey, raised scar.

I revisited physical therapy for a second course of treatment after radiation therapy when I was experiencing severe pain in my left shoulder joint, left arm and in all the ribs on the left side of my chest wall. This time I received deep tissue massage directly to the area followed by exercises to perform at home. This massage technique helped relieve my pain, restore mobility to my arm and, perhaps most beneficial of all, it relieved the repressed anger inside of me from my cancer diagnosis. It's essential to speak up to your oncologist about any muscle weakness, soreness, numbness, or tingling you may be feeling due to surgery to remove your cancerous tumor and lymph nodes. What you may be feeling is the beginning of lymphedema. Starting physical therapy, with a specifically trained lymphedema specialist, at the beginning of your cancer treatment may allow you to benefit from restoring full range of motion to your limbs.

PROPHYLACTIC SURGERY

I was just beginning to feel hopeful again after I completed my radiation therapy when I was called in for a follow up appointment with my gynecologist. I arrived feeling confident and healthy again. When, to my utter surprise, my doctor told me that I needed to seriously consider having my ovaries removed prophylactically. I was stunned at his announcement. I thought I was done with surgeries and treatment. He explained that my breast surgeon recommended removing the ovaries in premenopausal patients whose cancer was estrogen and/or progesterone receptor positive as a preventive measure against reoccurrence. He also recommended a total hysterectomy to guard against any other reproductive cancers that could develop if I chose to take a hormone inhibitor. Wow! This was a lot to digest in one appointment. I didn't feel hopeful at this moment. I felt sad and I felt angry. It reminded me of how quickly our hope can be squashed when we least expected it. After a good cry, I contacted my family and gave them the news. We all talked and tried to make sense of this next step in my journey.

Hope can be an elusive term. Sure, we feel hopeful after we've completed our cancer treatments. We feel elated. We feel ready to move on with our life or maybe to pick up our life where we left off before cancer so abruptly turned our world upside down. I can remember after an absence of a year due to my cancer treatments,

TRANSFORMATION

I bumped into some old colleagues at a networking dinner. They patted me on the back and looked intently into my eyes. Then one of them asked, "Everything's good, right? You're going to making it, right?" I remember pausing and thinking, "Am I going to make it?" I was hopeful that I was going to survive cancer and live a long life, but who really knows for sure. It was an odd question to ask a friend whose just emerged from a year of hell. Were they asking me this question because of their own fear of death? Did they need some reassurance of hope that if I lived and they would, too?

CHAPTER 3
FOOD

"To eat is a necessity, but to eat intelligently is an art."

~ Francois de La Rochefoucauld

This chapter focuses on four subtopics: super-foods, juicing vs. blending, understanding the role of sugar, and building back the immune system. Before I start advocating for healthy eating and creating an slightly alkaline environment in your body, I want to remind you that this book is about *transformation*. Before I took a wrong turn on the road and ended up in the land of cancer, I was known for having some very bad eating habits. I spent my childhood scraping the mixing bowl and licking the beaters after my mother baked homemade cookies. Later on, I would come home from a long day of teaching school and think nothing of devouring a half gallon of ice cream directly out of the tub. Even worse, when my children were out of the house, I'd spend a Saturday night watching television while stuffing 36 mini powdered sugar doughnuts down my throat. I never thought any of this mindless eating would ever catch up with me. On some level, I felt invincible as if only bad diseases happened to other people. Now I know better.

FEEDING YOUR BODY EXCEPTIONAL FOOD

First, begin by thinking of your body as your temple. Worship and feed your body as if your life depended on it. Your body has depended on what you have fed it along. It just that we didn't pay attention to it when we were feeling well and thriving and now we do. When you embrace the concept of living a truly exceptional life, you will become mindful of everything you put into your mouth. As Dr. Jan Chozen Bays stated in her book, *Mindful Eating: A Guide to Rediscovering a Healthy and Joyful Relationship with Food*, "Mindful eating is an experience that engages all parts of us, our body, our heart, and our mind, in choosing, preparing, and eating food."[4]

Now each morning when I wake up, I eagerly look forward to going downstairs to the kitchen and eyeing all the healthy food in my refrigerator. I asked myself, "What can I feed my body today that will build healthy bones and keep my immune system strong?" There is a feeling of satisfaction in knowing that I'm doing everything I can to take the best care of my body. Become pro-active in taking care of yourself. Focus on making smarter, healthier choices. Start by taking the time to study your food. Find out where it comes from and how it is made. By building relationships with your merchants, you will become more knowledgeable about where to find the highest quality, organically grown food available.

Meal planning and food preparation should be an enjoyable experience. Allow ample time to shop at various markets, learning to pair your drink with your main entree and to create a warm and inviting atmosphere in your kitchen for cooking and eating. To have an exceptional food experience use all of your senses while shopping, preparing, cooking and eating your food. For example, stock a variety of fresh, whole coffee beans in your pantry to choose from depending on your mood. Before grinding your beans, take a moment to breathe in the aroma of the coffee beans to prepare your body for the wonderfully, delicious taste of that first sip of coffee. Learn to value your relationship with your food.

SUPER-FOODS

Scientists have discover that certain foods, Super-foods, are rich in essential fatty acids, antioxidants or fiber which are vital to building a healthy body and a strong immune system. These foods have also been proven to lower total cholesterol, lower blood pressure, help protect against heart disease and cancer, help regulate blood sugar levels and metabolism and burn body fat. The process of converting your diet over from one of processed foods to one that contains mostly Super-foods can be daunting. As long as you are clear in your head that you are committed to giving up your old ways of eating, then you will succeed by putting imaginary blinders on your eyes whenever you see junk food. Instead, your eyes will twinkle with delight when they see heaps of beautiful, farm fresh fruits and vegetables. Below is the list of Super-foods and their benefits as recommended by Dr. Nicholas Perricone, a board certified nutritionist:[5]

1. Acai pulp, found in acai berries

The fatty acid content in açaí helps omega-3 fish oils penetrate the cell membrane; together they help make cell membranes more supple and efficient.

2. Allium - onions, garlic, leeks, shallots

Specifically, garlic lowers total cholesterol and blood pressure, lessening the risk of heart disease. It reduces the risk of blood clots. It also destroys infection-causing viruses and bacteria.

3. Barley

Eating hulled barley on a regular basis lowers blood cholesterol levels, protects against cancer and is also a good source of niacin, the B vitamin that is cardio-protective.

4. Beans and lentils

Beans and lentils, low in fat, calories and sodium but high in dietary fiber, are an excellent source of protein.

5. Buckwheat

The protein characteristics of buckwheat make it a cholesterol-lowering food. In addition, it reduces and stabilizes blood sugar levels - a key factor in preventing diabetes and obesity.

6. Green foods - wheat grass, spirulina

Green foods have beneficial effects on cholesterol, blood pressure, immune response and cancer prevention.

7. Hot peppers - sweet bell or hot chilis

Chilies are high in antioxidant carotenes and flavonoids, and contain about twice the amount of vitamin C found in citrus fruits.

8. Nuts and seeds

Nuts and seeds dramatically decrease your risk of cancer, heart disease and diabetes, and reduce the visible signs of aging like wrinkles and sagging skin.

9. Sprouts

Sprouts are a "living food" that continues to produce nutrients after being harvested. They are the most enzyme-rich food and they have a higher nutritional content than any other food.

10. Yogurt and kefir

Probiotic foods are primarily yogurt and kefir. They enhanced immune function, normalize immune responses, and may improve inflammatory conditions with an autoimmune component, such as asthma, eczema and Crohn's disease.

JUICING AND BLENDING

When I was first diagnosed with cancer, many people suggested that I start juicing. I had heard that juicing fruits and vegetables could provide benefits for the body, but I was somewhat skeptical. In my own research, I found that juicing is popular among those interested in alternative medicine. It is often used as an alternative means for fighting diseases such as cancer, strengthening cellular defense against free radicals, alleviating pain from migraines and decreasing the need for medication. Both juicing and blending are an easy way to get your daily servings of fruits and vegetables that otherwise would be difficult to eat.

Before I began chemotherapy, I asked my oncologist for her advice. She discouraged juicing because it works against the goal of chemotherapy which is the process of killing cancer cells. However, she was fine with juicing after completion of treatment. My curiosity led me to research the difference between juicing and blending. According to Jason Manheim's book, *The Healthy Green Drink Diet*, juicing contrasts from blending in the following ways:[6]

> Juicing provides both a quick nutritional boost and an energy boost. With all the fiber removed, the vitamins, enzymes and minerals in the juice enter your bloodstream

almost immediately allowing your body to feel instantly refreshed and revitalized. In addition, it's easily digestible without the bloating and heaviness.

Blending is a complete meal. It includes the vitamins, minerals, enzymes, all the fiber, protein and fats. Blending involves less sugar since less fruit is needed to produce one glass of juice. It's an easier cleanup since blending is a simple rinse-and-store.

I discovered in my reading that disease and destruction occurs more readily in a body that is mostly acidic. What does acidic mean? The human body is made up of 70% water, comprised of a wide range of solutions, which are either acid or alkaline. The pH of your body is a measure of the acidity or alkalinity of these solutions. The higher the pH reading, the more alkaline and oxygen-rich the fluid is. The lower the pH reading, the more acidic and oxygen-deprived the fluid is. A diet high in acidic-producing foods such as animal proteins, pasteurized dairy products, white sugar, caffeine, and processed foods puts pressure on the body's regulating systems to maintain pH neutrality. Because of this burden, an acidic body can suffer prolonged damage and degeneration resulting in disease. "To maintain health, it is recommended that a regular diet should consist of about 70% alkaline-forming foods and 30% acid-forming foods. If you are healing, whether you're battling a cold or a long-term disease, a restorative diet of 80% alkaline-forming foods to 20% acidic forming foods should be followed."[7] Greens such as spinach, kale, arugula, cabbage, broccoli, collards, chard and watercress, are very alkaline food. When greens are combined with fruits in either the juicing or blending process, they help regulate the blood to a healthier alkaline state.

I began juicing and blending after I had completed both chemotherapy and radiation therapy. My sister donated a Jack La Lanne power juicer to my cause. At first, I felt compelled to following recipes and shop for specific ingredients. After a few successful outings, I realized that I could experiment with creating my own juice drinks. This was when the fun really began! I stocked up on all kinds of seasonal fruits, frozen fruits, an assortment of greens and lemons, limes, ginger root, and mint leaves to give my juices an extra zing. I found that ripe fruits were the sweetest and most enjoyable in my drinks. Those were the ones I'd toss in the juicer with two or three handfuls of greens and another handful of baby carrots. I loved how the juice drinks made me feel vibrant, alive and alert.

As juicing became a part of my regular routine, clean up became a breeze. I learned to disassemble and assemble my power juicer in just five minutes. A word to the wise, don't delay in washing your juicer. Otherwise, the pulp remains start to dry out and you'll have a more difficult time scrubbing the juicer parts clean. Here are some tips on drinking your juice: Drink slowly and mindfully. Take time to chew your juice with each sip. Chew? Yes, sometimes your fresh juice comes out thick and needs to be chewed rather than slurped. This activates the secretion of saliva and enzymes that prep your body to absorb the nutrients that are in the juices.

UNDERSTANDING THE ROLE OF SUGAR

I'm convinced that sugar is evil. Not only did I lose my appetite for sugar while I was receiving chemotherapy, but it made me physically ill after my treatments were completed. Here's what I discovered about sugar in doing my own research. It depletes your immune system. Consuming sugar can decrease your white blood cells, inhibiting your body's ability to fight infection, viruses and disease. Sugar ages you faster. Consuming sugar causes free-radical damage and increases your risk for illness, disease and premature aging.

Sugar feeds candida. Candida is an overgrowth of a yeast fungus found in the intestines which can hinder the proper balance of good to bad flora and can spread throughout the body. Candida thrives on refined sugars and simple carbohydrates. In addition, refined sugar upsets your blood sugar levels and puts you at risk for diabetes and heart disease. Too much sugar increases your cortisol and estrogen hormones putting you at risk for developing breast cancer. Sugar is empty calories. It doesn't contain any vitamins or minerals. Sugar makes you overweight.

Finally, sugar can make you depressed. At first, sugar can increase serotonin, this is the neurotransmitter in your brain that makes you feel happy and elated. This initial high is followed by a low, a feeling of your energy crashing. Sugar becomes addictive as you crave sugar again wanting to re-create the high. Instead of eating sugar, focus on a whole foods diet filled with fruits, vegetables, nuts, seeds, and legumes. Eat protein with every meal to help curb your sugar cravings.[8]

Chemotherapy often causes many cancer patients to lose their appetite for just about everything including sugar. Other patients have spent a lifetime with a sweet tooth and have carried an extra thirty pounds around their waist, hips and thighs for most of their adult life. Trying every diet available, these patients never seem to get a handle on their sugar addiction until they are diagnosed with a serious illness. When they begin to understand sugar's role in the production of cancer cells, they will often search out alternative sweeteners that can help create a more alkaline environment in their bodies. Artificial sweeteners are not the answer.

TRANSFORMATION

Stevia, a plant based sweetener, is a perfect substitute for sugar because it is free of any harmful chemicals, easy to digest and is also available in a baking blend. Here are some other important facts about stevia:[9]

- Originally stevia grew wild in the highland region of Northern Paraguay and Southern Brazil. It was later cultivated for use as a sweetener until the introduction of sugar cane by the Spanish and Portuguese. Today stevia is grown around the world from China, Japan and other Asian countries to South America, Europe, India, the Ukraine and even North America.
- Stevia has been used since pre-Colombian times with no reports of ill side affects. Stevia has also withstood years of research that has proven stevia to be safe for human and animal consumption.
- Stevia is non-fermentable and therefore will not act as a food source for yeast. (This is why stevia is great for

anyone suffering from Candida.) Breads will still rise when baked but just not as big.

While I was undergoing chemotherapy, I was cooped up inside my house during the dead of winter. I decided to take on a project of modifying my baking recipes by substituting baking stevia whenever white or brown sugar was listed and infusing super-foods, like yogurt and walnuts, for added nutritional support. While I was revising my recipes, I learned few things about stevia that I'd like to pass on to others. There is a difference between raw stevia and the baking blend, which consists of a mixture of stevia leaf extract, erythritol, and a small amount of sugar. I found the stevia baking blend available in grocery stores under the brand name Truvia. In addition, I eliminated all glazes, frostings and icings from my recipes as my cakes, muffins and breads proved to be plenty sweet with the stevia sweetener. Finally, I learned to bake with the *unsweetened* version of coconut, chocolate and applesauce and my recipes still came out delicious in the end. Here are 15 recipes I'd like to share with you:

TRANSFORMATION

APPLE PECAN PIE

Apple pie is one of America's most beloved pies and marks nearly all American traditions. It's tasty aroma fills the atmosphere and brings a comfort to all who indulge. I've updated the traditional recipe by substituting stevia for sugar and adding chopped pecans for a heavenly taste. By using heart-shaped cookie cutters, I created a top crust with loving shapes that will draw anyone into the kitchen.

INGREDIENTS:

<u>For pie crust</u>:
3 cups all-purpose flour
1 teaspoon kosher salt
1 cup cold butter, cut into small pieces
1/4 to 1/2 cup ice water

<u>For apple pie filling</u>:
1/4 cup pecans, finely chopped
8 Granny Smith apples, peeled, cored and sliced
2 tablespoons lemon juice

FOOD

1/2 cup stevia, baking blend
2 tablespoons all-purpose flour
2 tablespoons cornstarch
1/4 teaspoon kosher salt
1 teaspoon ground cinnamon
1/4 teaspoon ground nutmeg
1/4 teaspoon allspice
1/2 cup boiled apple cider
2 tablespoons unsalted butter, diced

DIRECTIONS:

First, make the pie crust: Whisk together flour and salt in a large bowl. Using a pastry blender, cut in half the butter at a time. Then add the water, a tablespoon at a time, while tossing the mixture with a fork to moisten the dough evenly. Squeeze the dough gently to see if it will hold together. When it does, its moist enough. If it crumbles, add another tablespoon of water.

Turn out the dough onto a large piece of parchment paper. Gather it together by folding it once or twice. Divide the dough into two pieces, one for the bottom crust and one for the top crust. Flatten the dough into two round disks. Pat the edges to make them smooth, then wrap each disk in a plastic baggie and refrigerate for 30 minutes.

Unwrap your first dough disk and set on a piece of parchment paper. Cover the dough with a large piece of plastic wrap (this prevents the dough from sticking to the rolling pin). Roll the crust with a rolling pin from the center toward the outer edge. Roll the crust until it is 2 to 3 inches greater than the pie pan. Grease your pie pan lightly. Then transfer your pie crust to the pan by removing the plastic wrap and peeling back the parchment paper. To prevent a soggy bottom crust, brush the inside with a lightly beaten egg white. Then line the bottom crust with the finely chopped pecans.

Preheat oven to 425 degrees. Next, make the pie filling: In a large bowl, coat the sliced apples with the lemon juice. In a small bowl, whisk together stevia, flour, cornstarch, salt and spices. Sprinkle the mixture over the sliced apples and stir to coat them. Stir in the boiled apple cider. Spoon the apple filling onto the bottom crust on top of the pecans. Dot the top with diced butter. To finish the edge of your pie, fold the dough under to make it even with the rim of the pie pan. Then press it flat with the tines of a fork to give it a finished look.

Next, roll the top crust with a rolling pin between a piece of parchment paper and a piece of plastic wrap. Use heart shaped cookie cutters to cut hearts out of the dough. Layer the dough hearts side by side around the apple pie. When the pie filling is covered with hearts, gently brush the top crust with milk. Then sprinkle with stevia. Bake the pie for 20 minutes at 425 degrees, then reduce the oven temperature to 350 degrees and bake for 40 minutes more. Remove from oven and let the pie cool on a wire rack. Yields: one 9" double crust pie.

APPLESAUCE CAKE

INGREDIENTS:

1 1/2 cups all purpose flour
1 teaspoon baking soda
1/2 teaspoon kosher salt
3/4 teaspoon ground cinnamon

TRANSFORMATION

3/4 teaspoon ground nutmeg
1/4 teaspoon ground cloves
2 tablespoons flax seed
1/2 cup of raisins
1/2 cup of dried cranberries
1 cup of walnuts, chopped
1/2 cup of unsalted butter
1/2 cup of stevia, baking blend
2 tablespoons of honey
1 large egg
1 1/3 cups of unsweetened applesauce

DIRECTIONS:

Preheat the oven to 350 degrees. Grease and flour a Bundt pan. In a medium bowl, whisk together flour, baking soda, salt, spices and flax seed. In another bowl, toss together raisins, cranberries and nuts. In a large mixing bowl, cream together butter and stevia. Scrape down the bowl with a spatula. Beat in honey, egg and applesauce. Scrape down the bowl again with the spatula. Beat in the flour mixture in three parts. Finally, stir in the raisin/cranberry mixture.

Pour the batter into the prepared Bundt pan. Bake 40 to 45 minutes or until a toothpick inserted into the top of the cake comes out clean. Cool the cake in the pan on a wire rack for 15 minutes. Then insert a knife along the edge of the cake pan to loose the cake. Next, put a plate on top of the Bundt pan and flip the cake pan upside down. Let the cake continue to cool on the plate. Then slice cake into 1 inch servings and serve.

I made this delicious cake for the oncology nurses at the clinic where I received my chemotherapy infusions. They gobbled it up.

BANANA WALNUT BREAD

Banana walnut bread has always been one of my all time favorite quick breads. I love it toasted with a light spread of butter. It can be tricky to make as most of us have experienced the fated sunken top that ruins an otherwise perfect loaf of banana bread. I've received many requests for my recipe for Banana Walnut Bread. This recipe will send you back wanting slice after slice.

INGREDIENTS:

3/4 cup unsalted butter
3/4 cup stevia, baking blend
4 bananas, mashed

TRANSFORMATION

2 large eggs
1 teaspoon vanilla extract
2 cups all purpose flour
1 teaspoon baking soda
3/4 teaspoon salt
1/2 cup buttermilk
3/4 cup walnuts, chopped

DIRECTIONS:

Preheat oven to 325 degrees. Grease and flour a metal loaf pan. Cream the butter and stevia together thoroughly. Add the bananas, eggs and vanilla; beat well. Sift together flour, baking soda and salt. Mix flour mixture into the banana mixture, alternating with the buttermilk. Fold in the walnuts and mix well. Pour the batter into prepared loaf pan. Bake for 60 to 70 minutes, until toothpick inserted comes out clean. Let the bread cool in the pan for 15 minutes before turning it out onto a wire rack to cool completely.

Slice and toast lightly. Spread butter or preserves for an added treat.

BLUEBERRY LEMON MUFFINS

INGREDIENTS:

1/2 cup unsalted butter
1/2 cup stevia, baking blend
2 large eggs
2 tablespoons lemon juice
2 teaspoon lemon zest
1/2 cup milk
2 cups of all purpose flour
2 teaspoons baking powder
1/2 teaspoon kosher salt
2 cups blueberries, fresh or frozen

DIRECTIONS:

Preheat oven to 350 degrees. Grease muffin pan with nonstick spray. In a mixing bowl, cream together butter and stevia. Stir in eggs, milk, vanilla, lemon juice and zest. In a separate bowl, whisk together flour, baking powder and salt. Add flour mixture to the main mixing bowl in two additions. Carefully, fold in blueberries. Divide the batter into the muffin pan. Bake for 20 - 25 minutes. Remove from oven and let muffin pan cool for five minutes. Gently, remove muffins from the pan with a butter knife and continuing cooling on a wire rack for 15 more minutes. Yields: 12 muffins

BUTTERMILK CORNBREAD

INGREDIENTS:

1/2 cup unsalted butter, softened
1/3 cup stevia, baking blend
2 large eggs
1 cup buttermilk
1/2 teaspoon baking soda
1 cup cornmeal
1 cup all purpose flour
1/2 teaspoon kosher salt

DIRECTIONS:

Preheat oven to 375 degrees. Grease an 8 inch square pan. Combine butter and stevia and mix well. Add eggs and beat until well blended. In a separate bowl, combine buttermilk and baking soda together, then add to main bowl. Stir in cornmeal, flour, and salt until well blended. Pour batter into prepared pan.

Bake for 30 minutes or until toothpick inserted comes out clean. Cool on wire rack for 10 minutes. Remove from pan and continue to cool. Cut square into 9 servings.

CARROT WALNUT CRANBERRY MUFFINS

Here's my recipe for Carrot Walnut Cranberry Muffins, a perfect side to bowl of chili or cup of warm apple cider. These Fall muffins are chock-full of walnuts, cranberries, carrots, yogurt and oats making them a healthy choice, too.

INGREDIENTS:

2 cups all purpose flour
1 cup raw oats
1 tablespoon baking powder
1/2 teaspoon baking soda
1/2 teaspoon kosher salt
1/2 cup stevia, baking blend
1 teaspoon ground cinnamon
1/2 teaspoon ground nutmeg
2 large eggs

TRANSFORMATION

1/2 cup vegetable oil
1 1/2 cups plain greek yogurt
1 teaspoon vanilla extract
1 cup carrots, grated
1/3 cup dried cranberries
1/2 cup walnuts, chopped

DIRECTIONS:

Preheat the oven to 350 degrees. Grease a 12 muffin cup pan. Sift together flour, oatmeal, baking powder, baking soda, salt, cinnamon, nutmeg and stevia. In a large mixing bowl, mix together eggs, oil, yogurt, and vanilla. Stir in carrots, then dry ingredients in two additions. Fold in walnuts and cranberries. Spoon into muffin cup pan.

Bake for 25 minutes or until toothpick inserted comes out clean. Remove pan from oven and cool on a wire rack for 10 minutes. Use a butter knife to lift the muffins out of the pan. Cool completely before storing in an air tight container. This recipe also contains two of the Super-foods: walnuts and yogurt.

FOOD

CHEWY MOLASSES COOKIES

INGREDIENTS:

2 cups all purpose flour
1 1/2 teaspoons baking soda
1 teaspoon ground cinnamon
1/2 teaspoon ground nutmeg
1/2 teaspoon kosher salt
1/2 cup stevia, baking blend
3/4 cup unsalted butter, softened
1 large egg
1/4 cup molasses

DIRECTIONS:

Preheat oven to 350 degrees. Lightly grease the baking sheet. In a medium bowl, whisk together flour, baking soda, cinnamon, nutmeg and salt. In a large mixing bowl, beat butter and stevia until combined. Beat in egg and molasses. On low, gradually mix in dry ingredients in three parts.

In a small bowl, put 1/4 cup of stevia. Roll dough into 1 tablespoon balls. Then roll balls in stevia to coat before arranging them on the baking sheet three inches apart. Use the bottom of a glass to flatten the balls before baking. Bake 10 to 12 minutes. Cool 1 minute on baking sheet, then transfer the cookies to a wire rack to cool completely. Yields: 2 dozen. This recipe can be doubled if more cookies are desired.

CHOCOLATE CHUNK COOKIES

INGREDIENTS:

1 cup unsalted butter, softened
3/4 cup of stevia, baking blend
2 large eggs
1 1/2 teaspoons vanilla extract
1/2 teaspoon baking soda
1/2 teaspoon kosher salt
1 cup all purpose flour
2 1/4 cups raw oats
1 1/2 cups unsweetened coconut, shredded
8 ounces unsweetened chocolate squares, cut into 1/4 inch chunks
3/4 cup pecans, chopped

DIRECTIONS:

Preheat oven to 375 degrees. In a large mixing bowl, beat together butter and stevia until fluffy. Add eggs and beat until just blended. Then beat in vanilla, baking soda, and salt. Add flour and mix at low speed until just blended. Stir in oats, coconut, chocolate, and pecans.

Arrange 1 tablespoon mounds of cookie dough approximately three inches apart on greased cookie sheet. Then using the bottom of a glass, gently pat down each mound. Bake in the middle of the oven for 10 to 12 minutes. Cool cookies on pan for 1 minute. Then transfer to wire racks and cool for another 10 minutes. Store in an air tight container.

LEMON POUND CAKE

The first time I made this cake, I served it with a side of fruit salad. However, my guests all chose to put their scoop of fruit salad directly on their slice of pound cake as if it were strawberry shortcake.

INGREDIENTS:

1 1/2 cups all purpose flour
1/4 teaspoon baking soda
1/4 teaspoon kosher salt
3/4 cup unsalted butter
1/2 cup stevia, baking blend

TRANSFORMATION

1 1/2 teaspoons vanilla extract
1 teaspoon finely grated lemon zest
2 tablespoons fresh lemon juice
2 large eggs
1/2 cup sour cream
1/2 cup walnuts, chopped

DIRECTIONS:

Preheat oven to 325 degrees. Grease and flour loaf pan, preferably glass. In a medium bowl, whisk together flour, baking soda, and salt. Set aside.

In a large mixer bowl, beat together butter, stevia, vanilla extract, lemon zest, and lemon juice. Add the eggs, one at a time, mixing well. Add the sour cream, mix until blended. Then add the flour mixture in two parts, mix until blended. Finally, fold in the chopped walnuts.

Pour the batter into the prepared loaf pan. Bake 70 minutes, then check with a toothpick for doneness. Cool for 15 minutes in loaf pan. Run a knife around the inside of the pan, invert the cake onto a wire rack. Continue cooling for another 15 minutes. Finally, slice the cake into 1 inch slices and display slices on a rectangle tray.

MARBLE CHEESECAKE

INGREDIENTS:

For the Cheesecake:
3 (8oz.) packages cream cheese, softened
1/2 cup stevia, baking blend, divided
1/2 cup dairy sour cream
2 1/2 teaspoon vanilla extract, divided
3 tablespoons all purpose flour
3 large eggs
1/4 cup cocoa
1 tablespoon vegetable oil

For Chocolate Crumb crust:
2 cups graham cracker crumbs, crushed
1/2 cup cocoa
1/3 cup butter, melted
1/4 cup stevia, baking blend

DIRECTIONS:

Preheat oven to 350 degrees. To prepare chocolate crumb crust, combine graham cracker crumbs with stevia, cocoa, and melted butter. Press mixture into the bottom of a 10-inch springform pan. Bake 8 minutes. Cool completely.

Increase oven temperature to 450 degrees. To prepare the cheesecake, beat the cream cheese, 1/4 cup, plus 2 tablespoons stevia, sour cream and 2 teaspoons of vanilla extract in a large mixing bowl. Gradually add flour, beat until just blended. Add eggs, one at a time, beat well. Set aside.

In a separate bowl, combine cocoa and 2 tablespoons stevia. Then add oil, remaining 1/2 teaspoon vanilla extract and 1 1/2 cups of cream cheese mixture from above. Stir well. Next, alternately spoon plain and chocolate batters over baked chocolate crust, ending with the chocolate batter on top; gently swirl a knife through the batters for a marbled effect.

Bake the cheesecake for 10 minutes at 450 degrees. Without opening the oven door, reduce oven temperature to 250 degrees and continue baking 30 more minutes. Turn oven off. Without opening the oven door, leave cheesecake in the oven for 30 more minutes.

Remove from oven. Immediately loosen cheesecake from side of pan with a knife. Cool to room temperature. Refrigerate several hours or overnight. Remove the side of pan. Yields: 10 to 12 servings. Cover and refrigerate leftover cheesecake.

MOIST PUMPKIN BREAD

Pumpkins are low in calories and high in beta-carotene, an antioxidant that your body uses as Vitamin A. Did you know that pumpkins are 90% water. During their growth peak, usually August, giant pumpkins can gain as much as 40 lbs. per day.[10] Below is a recipe I created for a moist pumpkin bread without the calories of sugar.

INGREDIENTS:

1/2 cup stevia, baking blend
2 large eggs
1/2 cup vegetable oil
1/3 cup water
1 (15 ounce) pumpkin puree

TRANSFORMATION

1 3/4 cups all purpose flour
1 teaspoon baking soda
1/2 teaspoon baking powder
1 teaspoon kosher salt
1/4 teaspoon ground nutmeg
1 teaspoon ground cinnamon
1/4 teaspoon ground cloves
3/4 cup walnuts, chopped

DIRECTIONS:

Preheat oven to 325 degrees. Grease and flour a loaf pan (8.5 x 4.5). Set aside. In a medium size bowl beat eggs and mix in stevia, oil, water and pumpkin. In a separate bowl mix flour, baking soda, baking powder, salt, nutmeg, cinnamon and cloves. Combine wet ingredients with dry ingredients until just blended. Fold in chopped walnuts.

Pour batter into loaf pan. Bake for 50 to 60 minutes or until toothpick inserted comes out clean. Cool bread inside loaf pan for 10 minutes on a wire rack. Then slide a butter knife along the sides of pan to loosen the bread. Carefully invert the loaf pan to remove bread. Cool bread another 15 minutes directly on wire rack. Using a serrated knife, slice the pumpkin bread into 1/2 inch slices. Serve on a platter or store in an air tight container.

PEANUT BUTTER COOKIES

One of my favorite pastimes is sipping English tea and eating cookies. Even better is dunking those yummy, homemade cookies in my afternoon tea. Now that I've converted to using stevia when baking my cookies, there is a lot less guilt enjoying this childhood pastime. Here's my recipe for Peanut Butter cookies:

INGREDIENTS:

1/2 cup unsalted butter
5 tablespoons stevia, baking blend
1 large egg
1 teaspoon vanilla extract
1 cup peanut butter, chunky style
1 1/4 cups all purpose flour
1/4 teaspoon baking soda
1/2 teaspoon kosher salt
Additional 2 tablespoons stevia for crosshatch pattern

# TRANSFORMATION

DIRECTIONS:

Preheat oven to 350 degrees. In a large mixing bowl, beat together butter and stevia. Beat in egg, vanilla extract and peanut butter, scraping down the bowl frequently. Place a sifter over the mixing bowl. Sift and stir the flour, salt, and baking soda in the mixing bowl. Using a medium size cookie scooper, make 2 teaspoon size balls. Set them on a baking sheet lined with parchment paper, approximately two inches apart. Dip a fork into a separate bowl of stevia, then press a crosshatch pattern into the top of each dough ball. Bake the cookies 12 to 13 minutes. Cool on baking sheet 2 minutes, before removing to wire rack. Makes 2 dozen.

PECAN PIE TARTS

INGREDIENTS:

For Crust:
8 ounces cream cheese, softened
1 1/4 cup unsalted butter, softened
2 1/2 cup all purpose flour

For Filling:
1/4 cup unsalted butter, softened
3/4 cup stevia, baking blend
2 large eggs
2 teaspoons vanilla extract
1 1/2 cup pecans, chopped
1/3 cup unsweetened shredded coconut
1/2 cup dried dates, chopped

DIRECTIONS:

Preheat oven to 325 degrees. Grease 12 muffin cups and set aside. In a mixing bowl, cream together cream cheese and butter until light and fluffy. Blend in flour, 1/2 cup at a time. Roll into 12 balls. Press one ball into each muffin cup, lining the bottom and sides like a pie crust.

In a medium mixing bowl, cream together 1/4 cup butter and stevia until light and fluffy. Beat in eggs and vanilla until thoroughly blended. Stir in pecans, coconut and dates. Fill each tart cup almost to the top. Bake for 25 minutes. Let the tarts cool in the muffin pan, then use the end of a table knife to loosen tarts from the pan. Store in a air tight container.

PISTACHIO BISCOTTI

INGREDIENTS:

1 cup pistachios, shelled and lightly toasted
1/2 cup unsalted butter
3 large eggs
1/2 cup of stevia, baking blend
1 teaspoon vanilla extract
3 1/4 cups of all purpose flour
1 teaspoon baking powder
1/2 teaspoon kosher salt

DIRECTIONS:

Preheat the oven to 350 degrees. In large mixing bowl, beat the butter until light and fluffy. Gradually add in the eggs, stevia and vanilla extract until creamy. Add the flour, baking powder and the salt. Use a wooden spoon to mix in the pistachios.

Transfer the dough onto a lightly floured surface. Cut in half. Roll each half into a log, approximately 12 inches long by 1 inch high. Place the logs onto a lightly greased cookie sheet and bake for 30 minutes. Let the logs cool for 5 minutes. Place onto a cutting board and slice each log into 1 inch thick slices. Place the cookie slices back on the cookie sheet and bake 5 minutes. Turn the cookies over and bake another 5 minutes. Cool the cookies on a wire rack. Then store them in an airtight container.

ZUCCHINI BREAD WITH WALNUTS AND YOGURT

Here's a sugar free recipe for Zucchini bread that includes two of the Super-foods - walnuts and yogurt. You'll find the greek yogurt keeps this bread moist for up to four days. So go ahead and make it, substituting stevia for sugar, and you'll enjoy this sweet bread all week long.

INGREDIENTS:

1 cup walnut halves
2 cups all purpose flour
1/2 teaspoon baking powder
1/2 teaspoon baking soda
1/2 teaspoon kosher salt
1/2 cup stevia, baking blend
2 large eggs
1/2 cup of vegetable oil

TRANSFORMATION

1/2 cup plain Greek yogurt
1 cup zucchini, coarsely grated

DIRECTIONS:

Preheat oven to 325 degrees. Butter and flour a metal loaf pan, set aside. In a medium bowl, whisk the flour with the baking powder, baking soda, and salt. In a large mixing bowl, mix the stevia with the eggs, vegetable oil and yogurt. Add the dry ingredients to the wet ingredients, along with the grated zucchini and walnuts. Stir until the batter is evenly moistened.

Scrape the batter into the loaf pan. Bake 70 minutes or until a toothpick inserted into the center of the loaf comes out clean. Let the loaf cool on a rack for 30 minutes. Slice into 1 inch slices and serve with butter and preserves.

BUILDING BACK THE IMMUNE SYSTEM

In my quest to rebuild my immune system after my cancer treatments, one of my doctor suggested I eat beef liver. Initially, I was aghast at the thought of eating liver. Like so many people,

FOOD

I'd been scarred as a child with the smell of liver cooking on the stove top. My mother, who was anemic, regularly cooked beef and chicken livers to boost her iron levels. She also bought other organ meat, like cow's tongue, intestines, and other unsightly things and stored them in our freezer. When my doctor recommended that I eat liver, I realized it was time for me to get over my hang up and research how to make liver taste good.

First, make sure to buy pasture-feed, hormone-free beef liver. Second, sauté it with chopped onions, minced garlic, and bacon. The bacon flavor will kill the bad smell and make the liver taste good. Finally, add 1/2 cup of Sauvignon Blanc wine to the pan and cook the liver for 15 or 20 minutes, or until the liver is medium well with a little pink color. The beef liver will smell like a gourmet entree and taste good, too.

Beef liver is loaded with essential vitamins, minerals and other nutrients our bodies need. The reason it's the recommended food for rebuilding your blood cells and improving your immune system is because of its high levels of iron, folate, and vitamins A,

TRANSFORMATION

D, and B12. For example, when compared to blueberries, kale, and ordinary beef, liver has 53,400 IU of vitamin A, 19 IU of vitamin D, 8.8 mg of iron, 145 micrograms of folate and 111 mg of vitamin B12 in one serving measuring 100 grams.[11] The only disadvantage of eating liver is that it's high in cholesterol.

CHAPTER 4
HEALTH & FITNESS

"A wise man should consider that health is the greatest of human blessings, and learn how by his own thought to derive benefit from his illnesses."

~ **Hippocrates**

HOW TO FIND EXCEPTIONAL HEALTHCARE

It's our job to be our own healthcare advocate. We can not and should not expect anyone else to do this for us. It's imperative that we become an active member of our medical team at all times during our life, but especially so during a diagnosis of cancer. The way that we find exceptional healthcare is by asking questions, seeking second opinions, doing our own research, and by voicing our opinion regarding our own diagnosis and treatment plan. There are Patient's Bill of Rights. One of our rights is the right to refuse a recommended treatment at any time during our plan of care. Don't be afraid of your doctor. Focus on being kind, considerate and assertive when you interact with your medical team. Be sure to ask for a hard copy of all of your pathology reports, lab results, consent forms, radiation doses and a list of all the chemo drugs that were given to you during your infusions. This is important because delayed side effects can arise several years later from your initial diagnosis and treatment.

While I was going through radiation therapy, I met a woman who was also a breast cancer patient. She told me that she never looked at her body below the neck when she saw herself in the mirror. Eleven years before she was diagnosed with cancer, she went to her doctor complaining that her breast hurt. Her doctor told her to stop drinking coffee and sodas, but never performed a breast exam or a mammogram because she wasn't insured. Instead of insisting on a breast exam, she just left the doctor's office and went home. More than a decade later, her husband noticed a dent going across her left breast and told her she should have it checked out. That's when she found out she had Stage III breast cancer. This is a perfect example of a passive patient.

When you become an active patient seeking good medical care, you maximize your chances for recovery, keeping yourself as pain-free and functional as possible. Exceptional healthcare requires that you put in the time and energy required to be an active patient and in doing so you are in a better position to enjoy life. There are many options available to you as a patient. If the medication your doctor has given you is not working, then you need to ask for something different. There is no excuse for anyone to suffer needlessly.

WESTERN VS. EASTERN MEDICINE

Western medicine encompasses all types of conventional medical treatment, including surgery, chemotherapy, radiation, and physical therapy performed by doctors, nurses and other conventional healthcare providers. It differs from Eastern or alternative medicine in that it relies heavily upon industrially produced medication and a strict adherence to the formal scientific process. On the other hand, "complementary" and "alternative" are terms used to describe a number of products, practices, and systems that are not part of mainstream Western medicine. They can include things like herbs and dietary supplements, body movement, spiritual approaches, extracts, and creams or ointments. The *American Cancer Society* considers complementary and alternative medicine to be different from each other[12]:

- Alternative medicine is used <u>instead</u> of standard or mainstream medical treatment, often with serious outcomes for the patient.
- Complementary medicine is used <u>along</u> with mainstream medical care. If carefully chosen and properly used, some of these can improve your quality of life without causing problems with your regular cancer treatment.

HEALTH & FITNESS

CANCER: A COMPLEMENTARY APPROACH

By Dr. Ann Losee

Years ago, before I went to school to study Traditional Chinese Medicine, I came across the book *Between Heaven and Earth: A Guide To Chinese Medicine*, by Efram Korngold and Harriet Beinfeld. Below is a very important quote that explains Chinese Medicine succinctly and beautifully: "Within Chinese cosmology, all of creation is born from the marriage of two polar principles, *Yin* and *Yang*: *Earth* and *Heaven*, winter and summer, night and day, cold and hot, wet and dry, inner and outer, heavy and light, body and mind. The harmony of this union means health, good weather, and good fortune, while disharmony can mean disease, disaster, and bad luck. The strategy of Chinese medicine is to restore harmony. Each human being is seen as a world in miniature, a garden in which doctor and patient together strive to cultivate health. Every person has a unique terrain to be mapped, a resilient yet sensitive ecology to be maintained. As the gardener uses methods such as irrigation and compost to grow vigorous plants, the doctor uses acupuncture, herbs, and food to recover and sustain health."[13]

Allopathic medicine tends to look at the human body as a machine, with individual parts operating to benefit the whole. A doctor can therefore be viewed as a mechanic, who can figure out what is broken and why the body isn't working smoothly. If I were to break an arm, I would want to visit a doctor to help me reset it. The downside to this approach in allopathic medicine is that the individual gets compartmentalized and patients are sent from specialist to specialist, without any connection to the whole. It is my view that both approaches are important, which is why I am a firm advocate for Integrative Medicine, which fuses the two.

In my clinic, I strive to look at where the imbalances lie and do my best to help the body move back into balance. I may use any of the following modalities to achieve the best effect: acupuncture, moxibustion or cupping therapy, nutritional and food guidance, Chinese herbal medicine, supplemental therapy, Qi Gong or other exercise guidance, Reiki or healing touch, and essential oil therapy. In my experience, diet and lifestyle habits are a huge influence on disease and illness in the US. The patients who are most successful in gaining health are those who make appropriate lifestyle changes, such as quitting smoking or drinking, eating less sugar and processed foods, exercising regularly, and incorporating meditation or prayer into their daily lives.

Regarding cancer, I use this complementary approach to help my patients with side effects from chemotherapy and radiation therapy. Most recent studies on cancer and acupuncture show it to be helpful for nausea, pain, and other symptoms associated with chemotherapy. Acupuncture can help improve the quality of life in cancer patients. It is important for me to stress that acupuncture cannot cure cancer. It is best when used as an adjunct to allopathic treatments. In addition, Qi Gong and Tai Chi, which are ancient martial art techniques, can be used to help cancer patients. A recent study conducted by the National Cancer Institute and MD Anderson Cancer Center has shown medical Qi Gong to be helpful in lowering depression and improving quality of life in patients undergoing radiation treatment for breast cancer.[14]

I've used several complementary treatments from Eastern Medicine, and successfully achieve a decrease in the side effects from my surgeries, chemotherapy and radiation therapy. It's important to check with your traditional doctor first before you decide to use any treatments within Eastern Medicine. Below is a list of my treatments, along with a brief description and the benefits I received.

<u>Imagery</u> - is the use of visualization techniques designed to enable the mind to influence the health and well being of the

body. I found imagery very useful during my diagnostic testing when I underwent numerous MRIs and CT scans. I also found it to be effective in reducing my fear during radiation therapy, while imagining the radiation beam to be a healing light.

<u>Massage</u> - involves the manipulation, rubbing, and kneading of the body's muscles and soft tissues with the use of oils, aromatherapy and soothing music. With each session of massage therapy I received, I experienced a decrease in my anxiety, depression, and bone pain.

<u>Polarity therapy</u> - is a system of touch and movement using the positive and negative charges of the body's electromagnetic energy field. Polarity was effective in restoring the balance of the natural flow of energy throughout my body.

<u>Reiki</u> - is a form of treatment used to manipulate energy fields within and around the body to liberate the body's natural healing powers. It can be given in either a hands-on or hands-off format. Reiki is a Japanese word meaning "universal life energy." Reiki was helpful in relieving my anxiety and allowing me to experience complete relaxation.

TRANSFORMATION

Acupuncture - is a technique in which very thin needles of varying lengths are inserted through the skin to treat a variety of conditions. Acupuncture was extremely effective in treating my nausea caused by chemotherapy drugs and in relieving bone and muscle pain during both chemotherapy and radiation therapies.

Aromatherapy - is the use of fragrant substances distilled from plants, essential oils, to alter moods or improve health. They can be inhaled or diluted with olive oil and applied to the skin. I found peppermint oil to be effective in reducing the intensity of my hot flashes. I also found lavender oil to be effective in reducing anxiety and promoting relaxation.

Yoga - is a form of exercise that involves a program of precise poses and breathing activities to create a union of mind, body, and spirit. Yoga was effective in building my core strength, restoring balance, relaxation and physical fitness.

Feng Shui - is the ancient Chinese philosophy of placing physical objects to promote the beneficial flow of vital energy or life force call chi and to allow humankind to live in harmony with the environment and the universe. I implemented the five elements of Feng Shui ~ Wood, Fire, Earth, Metal and Water ~ when I constructed the Wellness Garden in my back yard. This garden became my sanctuary of healing during my cancer recovery.

<u>Art Therapy</u> - is a form of treatment used to help people with physical and emotional problems by using creative activities to express emotions. It provides a way for people to express unspoken and often unconscious concerns about their illness. While I was going through cancer treatments a friend of mine, who was also suffering from multiple illnesses, would get together with me regularly for art therapy sessions. We both benefitted from this creative outlet. You can also find workshops on healing through music, art and journaling available through your local hospital cancer center network.

WHY FITNESS IS IMPORTANT TO AN EXCEPTIONAL LIFE

Before I was diagnosed with cancer, I never had a regular exercise regimen. I would take random walks, maybe for 30 minutes, around the neighborhood once or twice a week. These walks were usually initiated when I felt guilty about over indulging in a dessert or after I spent an afternoon eating cookie dough. I never exercised for pleasure or to maintain a fit body.

A year before my diagnosis, I became curious about yoga. I started attending beginning yoga classes twice a week and found that I enjoyed the experience because it kept my arthritis at bay and it didn't require much sweating. I continued to attend yoga actively during my diagnosis, surgery and chemotherapy because of the mind-body connection. Yoga gave me clarity and purpose in my life. It also helped alleviate some of the nausea associated with the chemotherapy. When chemotherapy started to make me dizzy during yoga class, I immediately found a substitute form of exercise that kept my head upright. I started jogging on the treadmill, followed by 30 minutes of light weight lifting. Eventually, I added twenty minutes on the elliptical trainer three times a week. For the first time in my life, I committed to exercising on a regular basis because I enjoyed the workouts and looked forward to the positive side effects of exercising: a better attitude, decreased depression, weight management, and increased muscle tone.

Exercise is important to an exceptional life because it promotes good health and life balance. While we are pursuing our passions and eating a healthy diet, we must find time in our weekly schedule for regular exercise at least three to five days a week. If you can't think of how to exercise, then start by walking your neighborhood three times a week for thirty minutes at a time. There are many facilities in your community that offer classes and a complete weight resistance gym. Call your local community center, WMCA or fitness club. Here you will find adult classes in yoga, Zumba, spinning, tai chi, and swimming. Seniors, over 50 years old, usually receive a discounted price so you can easily incorporate a few classes a week into your schedule for a nominal fee.

Consider joining a local bowling or bocce ball team. Not only will you benefit from exercise but you'll also make new friends. My Father, a cancer survivor who is well into his seventies, has always enjoyed bicycling. He belongs to two bicycling clubs which keep

TRANSFORMATION

him cycling three times a week anywhere from 45 to 60 miles each time. In addition, these clubs plan weekend outings and camping trips which have enabled him to enjoy a full social life, too. If you've spent a good portion of your adult life as a couch potato, then it's time to make a permanent lifestyle change by committing to getting yourself out of that old rut and get moving. By doing so you will become the example for your spouse, your children and everyone around you.

CHAPTER 5
BEAUTY

"Everything has beauty, but not everyone sees it."

~ **Confucius**

BEAUTY AND CANCER

During my chemotherapy treatment, I lost not only the hair on my head but all of my body hair. After I lost the hair on my arms and legs, I develop a sensitivity to cold temperatures. This sensitivity was intensified by the fact that I was going through chemo during the winter months when temperatures were dipping down below 20 degrees at night. I distinctly remember bathing in the shower one day when I happen to look down and realized that I had also lost all of my pubic hair! I let out a scream because my body was now completely naked of all hair, including my eyelashes and eyebrows.

Before all of my hair fell out, my finger nails became discolored with an ugly brown haze and some of my nails began to lift. I tried my best to keep my nails trimmed and mostly out of sight from the public. Fortunately, I didn't lose any of my fingernails. Additional, during my chemo treatment, the skin on both my hands and my feet peeled completely off. It was quite ugly, but thankfully my oncologist suggested using Aquaphor cream which relieved this unsightly side effect.

My chemotherapy treatment took five months to complete. As I watched my physical appearance change from a vibrant woman to an unrecognizable alien, I began to contemplate the topic of beauty and all the pressure that society puts on a woman to maintain a physically attractive appearance. For me, I began using cosmetics at the age of twelve. Followed by hair color at the age of 28. In my thirties, my beauty routine expanded to include manicures, pedicures and massages. In my forties, I began to straighten and highlight my hair and added brow waxes and facials to my beauty regimen. By the time I turned 51, I had spent hundreds of hours sitting in beauty salons and thousands of dollars on beauty treatments. I did this because I thought it would make me happy and I thought others would find me attractive.

I began to ask myself why? Would I go back to such an intense beauty regimen or would I feel confident enough to be my own person and create a more liberated routine? With no body hair anywhere, I was now saving both time and money and was able to focus my energy on more constructive activities. However, when I looked at my reflection in the mirror, I hardly recognized the woman staring back at me. She looked plain and androgynous, but I knew it was really me on the inside. I also despised the scars from my surgeries that seem to stand out like medals hard earned from my war against cancer. Every night, I coated them with Vitamin E cream in hopes of getting them to fade faster. I pondered further whether a man would find me attractive enough to sustain a relationship? While I was traveling to California to visit my family, I had a layover at the Los Angeles International airport. I was enjoying a brief respite at a sports bar, when in walked five young women all with different shades of long, blond hair. I watched as they talked and laughed and flipped their hair all around. I was secretly envious of them as I cringed even further underneath my synthetic wig. I thought to myself, "Is beauty fake blond hair, spray-on tans and heavy make up?" They were certainly attractive women, but at what cost? Could I find beauty with a more natural look? It was then that I asked my dear friend Shannon to share her definition of beauty.

WHAT DEFINES BEAUTY?

By Shannon Hoskovec

I grew up hearing and eventually believing that I was ugly. I didn't understand what beauty was, but I did know that it wasn't what was reflected when I stood in front of a mirror. So I never gave much thought to how I treated

BEAUTY

this ugly body. Only beautiful things were to be cared for, admired, held in esteem.

It wasn't until I began to see what beauty really is. I live in the mountain deserts of New Mexico. On more than one occasion, I have been stopped still at the wonder of the setting sun and all the golden glorious colors that set the horizon aflame. This is what beauty does – completely suspends us in time and fills us with pleasure. Beauty is an experience.

As I began to be open to the beauty that surrounds me in nature – the sky, stars, phases of the moon, the brilliant flowers and exquisite animals, and even the myriad of people that dance into and out of my life, I saw that even this ugly body has beauty. Having such a treasure should be treated with care, and even admired, and held in esteem.

Beauty is displayed unhindered in nature and through nature's God. So I researched the best I could

TRANSFORMATION

give my skin, my hair, my body. This is where I look for my beauty needs. My body deserves the experience of life and beauty if for no other reason than God himself sees beauty in me. Pure beauty has its foundations deep within the body. Here, where the singularly complex cell lives, begins the process that supports the body and gives beauty. When the cell is fed *life*, it breeds *life*. This life is the seed of beauty. I believe to have true beauty, you must consider the cell.

Any skin care product which support the cell, that gives the cell the nutrients and nourishment it needs, is fit for the body. Any products which have Parabens, unnatural chemicals, or are otherwise detrimental to the cell are fit for the trash bin. Since I require products that I apply topically as well as take internally to be nourishing to my cells, I researched and considered many products and companies, and I finally found a company whose products meet both my needs and my expectations. I may spend a bit more on the products, but I use far less. That which I do use supports my cells and my beauty. I can now experience true beauty.

HAIR CARE

Losing your hair during cancer treatment can be very upsetting. For many women, hair loss is the most traumatic side effect of chemotherapy. Some women even decline chemotherapy due to the fear of hair loss. I can reassure you that hair loss due to cancer treatment is usually temporary. There are many creative ways to deal with hair loss: wigs, turbans, scarves and hats. Save a clip of your own hair before you start chemotherapy so you'll be able to match the color if you decided to get a wig.

Wigs can create the look of thick, healthy-looking hair. There are two types: ready-made synthetic wigs or custom-made human hair wigs. The cost of one wig can be between $150 - $1,000. I recommend doing some comparison shopping by trying on several styles and types before you decide on one. Your local American Cancer Society office may be able to provide you with a donated wig for free. Otherwise, call your health insurance company and inquire about reimbursement for a cranial prothesis. This is the term the insurance industry uses for providing a cancer patient with a wig. Most insurance companies provided coverage in the amount of $300 to $500 for reimbursement of a wig. Save your receipts and have your wig provider signed the appropriate insurance form.

When I first learned that I would lose my hair, I asked a friend who had been through chemotherapy to accompany me to the wig shop. When we arrived at the store, I was amazed at how many styles and colors there were to choose from. Each wig had its own name - Helena, Nicole, Kristina and so on. I decided to have a little fun by trying on wigs with straight hair and highlights. Having had naturally curly hair all my life, I had always dreamed of what it would feel like to have perfectly straight hair that fell into place every time. I bought the 'Heather' wig and proudly wore it home, checking to see if other drivers noticed my new look. Over the course of six months of baldness, I received so many compliments and stares wearing that wig that many people suggested that I consider styling my new hair growth in the same way. I have to admit that wearing a wig simplified my daily beauty routine in a dramatic way. No more blow dryers, curling irons, flat irons, fancy clips and hairspray. I could pull my whole look together in five minutes!

Once my new hair grew back, thick and healthy, my oncologist allowed me to color my hair. After twenty-five years of damaging my hair with toxic commercial hair dyes, I made a decision to only use the purest hair color I could find. That's when I discovered Organic Color Systems made of certified organic extracts, natural ingredients and free of parabens. A friend referred me to the only certified organic salon in my town. My hair stylist, Nicole, shared with me the importance of using organic products.

In my profession, as a hair stylist, I've met many wonderful people, from doctors, writers, to stay-at-home moms. The ones that touch my heart the most are the ones who have survived cancer. These are the clients who want to change their everyday habits that could have contributed to their cancer so they can stay cancer free. Having had two grandmothers with breast cancer, I understand their desire for change.

Parabens are one of my biggest concerns when it comes to breast cancer. They are a class of chemicals widely used as preservatives by cosmetic and pharmaceutical industries. Parabens are effective preservatives in many types of formulas. They can be found in shampoos, commercial moisturizers, shaving gels, deodorants, spray tanning solutions, makeup and toothpaste. The problem is they can be absorbed through the skin, blood and digestive system. Studies have shown our lymph nodes seem to collect the parabens. When biopsies are performed on breast cancer patients, many times parabens are detected in small samples of the tumor. Given that over 40% of all breast tumors are found in the upper-outer quadrant of the breast, closest to the underarm, its more than likely that a link exists between parabens and cancer.

Today, I am a certified organic hair colorist. All the beauty services offered at the salon, including nails, hair, skin and body, use eco-friendly products from the United Kingdom. I get so much satisfaction out of knowing I can help women stay toxin free and look their best. I will do whatever I can to be a positive role model and live an organic and toxin free lifestyle. We can all make a difference by starting with ourselves.

~ **Nicole Kuhlmann**

Gambei Wellness Spa & Salon

CHAPTER 6
ATTITUDE & PASSION

"Attitude is a little thing that makes a big difference"

~ Winston Churchill

CHANGING PERCEPTIONS AND ATTITUDE

Cancer stigma refers to a negative perception of a person affected by cancer. Stigma can be internal; it can affect the self-perception of survivors, causing guilt, blame or shame. It can cause discrimination, loss of employment or income, or social isolation. Stigma thrives when misinformation and anxiety exist in a community where cancer awareness has not been taught. In the developing world, the stigma and mystery that surround cancer

TRANSFORMATION

is so great that the word "cancer" is rarely used and the disease is not talked about openly. When stigma, fear, and silence around cancer exist, more people succumb to cancer.

To move forward in a positive and uplifting way, we need to adjust our attitude toward cancer. The last thing a cancer patient needs is to feel isolated from friends or fear being left by a loved one. In many countries, the stigma surrounding cancer and the perception that cancer is a death sentence creates great social costs for patients. A survey conducted by the *Lance Armstrong Foundation* and highlighted at the *International Conference on Global Health* found that in nine countries, Japan, Mexico, Russia, Argentina, China, France, India, Italy and South Africa, 25% of the respondents believe cancer patients brought the disease on themselves. More than half of respondents in China and India agreed with the sentiment.[15]

Cancer can change us in so many ways, physically, emotionally and spiritually. I asked my friend Martha Powell to share how she turned her attitude around and pursued an exceptional life after her cancer diagnosis.

ATTITUDE & PASSION

A POSITIVE ALTITUDE

By Martha Powell

When I was asked to write a piece on a positive attitude during and after cancer I thought that writing about a positive **altitude** might be better. Taking a look at my elevation in life.

When diagnosed in 2000 with Non Hodgkin's Lymphoma, stage IV, my life's altitude was out of whack. I found it difficult to breathe. Just like a mountain climber, I found that it was a process of stamina. Going from base camp to the next camp and onward. Surviving the diagnosis was my first base camp, the beginning of the cancer survivor journey.

The climb of "Mt. Cancer" is new territory for most of us. Like climbers on Mt. Everest, there are guides (other survivors) and sherpas (care takers/family) who help carry our pack when it gets too heavy. At the end of my treatment, when I reached the peak, I had to prepare for the decent.

TRANSFORMATION

How does one cope with so much that has changed personally into a world where things appear to have remained the same for everyone else? Such is this journey.

For me, the positive altitude kept me going one day at a time until I could plan for one month at a time, to one year at a time and so forth. Now I seek to keep at the elevation that sustains a favorable life.

If our altitude is kept in the positive, it allows us to breathe, give us a clearer outlook and keeps us from going into a minus altitude where the pressures of life crushes our courage to continue on or from going to an altitude so high that the air is thin of dreams and aspirations. The positive altitude is where the air is filled with hope and life.

It does take work to be at the right altitude in life but is worth the effort. Life before the cancer experience may have seemed easier but it had it's challenges too. The difference now is that I know the bouquet of gratitude. That fragrance that says, "I am alive."

ATTITUDE & PASSION

Fast forward, it has been 13 years since my diagnosis and first treatments. In 2001 and 2004 I had recurrences. More treatment. Today I am in remission. I work on keeping my altitude in the positive. Staying at the right elevation helps me flourish as a survivor.

As a travel professional, I produce group cruises (Cancer Survivor Cruise, Wine Makers Cruise and others) and donate a portion of the proceeds to the NM Cancer Center Foundation. This helps gives a patient some breathing room in their altitude with needs beyond medical.

Some survivors prefer to separate their life from their cancer journey, treating the journey like a bad seed. At the right elevation, I believe this seed can spawn so many beautiful gifts; compassion, friendships, gratitude, love, and more.

Find your positive **altitude** and thrive!

WHAT'S YOUR PASSION?

Many cancer survivors experience their disease as a wake up call. They make dramatic changes to their diet and daily schedule

TRANSFORMATION

to accommodate a new exercise regimen. Others see their diagnosis as a second chance to embrace life and go after their passions. Living an exceptional life is about giving yourself permission to be fully engage in life doing whatever it is that excites you. There are so many avenues available to you to keep you happy in your survivorship: traveling, gardening, dancing, cooking, art classes, bicycling clubs, book clubs, wine tasting cruises, technology classes, horseback riding, volunteer work, or even getting involved with cancer research and fundraising. My neighbor, an eight year kidney cancer survivor, is completely happy in his retirement. He keeps active by doing what really excites him in life: car racing, woodworking, and playing golf with his buddies. Every time I see him he is fully engaged in life and not about to let his cancer diagnosis drag him down.

One of my passions is gardening and outdoor living. When I was sick with nausea and fatigue while going through chemotherapy, I decided to use my passion for gardening to design a Wellness Garden Retreat in my backyard. Although it was the middle of winter during my treatment, I used this time inside the house to draw my designs, research decking materials and to interview contractors. When spring arrived, I was ready to break ground. In my quest to create an exceptional garden, I designed a plan for both the front and back of my house that would allow me to soak in the natural beauty of the mountains coupled with plenty of deck space for relaxing and meditating.

The goal of my outdoor design was to create a retreat where I could heal from my cancer treatments and replenish my soul. I wanted to incorporated each of the Feng Shui elements: wood, earth, fire, metal and water. Construction began at the beginning of March when it was still snowing in the mountains. While contractors installed wood posts and built the form for the deck, I began to shop for the flowers, plants, furniture and other outdoor accessories. When construction was completed, I invited five friends over to help me plant flowers, spread wood chips, hang wind chimes and create a meandering path made from flagstone. Within two hours, we had transformed my backyard into a welcoming haven. Below is an example of how another cancer survivor is making the most of her passions:

PAY IT FORWARD

By Gayle Allen

Strong, courageous, full of hope, inspiring, hero... These are several words friends and family have used to describe me from the time I was diagnosed, on through the past 11 years since I've faced down cancer.

The truth be known, at the beginning, and several times during treatment, I felt the exact opposite of those words. Through the help of family, friends, my husband and my son, I only felt that way for a short time. I found that being strong became a way of getting through each day, even when I didn't really feel it inside. A cheery smile, kindness and compassion for others made being strong a way of life. As a famous quote says: "You don't know how strong you are until strong is your only choice." Strength and courage also came from staying close to other survivors, from whom I drew much hope and inspiration.

A cancer diagnosis very quickly reveals to us that life is not to be taken for granted, that each day must be treasured. To me, living a full life means not only enjoying each day for ourselves, but doing what we can to help others. Volunteer to sit with a patient, visit those who are homebound, help the needy - honor those who have helped you by paying it forward. My biggest joy now is working to help bring awareness for early detection, and raising funds to enable researchers to find the cure for cancer. I've spent the last 6 years staying heavily involved in the American Cancer Society's Relay For Life event and their Reach to Recovery program. All of these things, and more, are what gives life meaning.

DEVELOPING YOUR BUCKET LIST

In talking with many cancer survivors, I discovered that some of them have no drive, ambition, or direction. They are simply

TRANSFORMATION

existing from one medical appointment to the next. They have allowed their cancer diagnosis to dominate their daily life and in doing so I believe they may be setting themselves up for reoccurrence. This is not exceptional life to live. This is a doomed existence. In creating your new life post-cancer, its important to develop a Bucket List of goals for your life. This list can include activities you want to accomplish and/or places you want to visit so that you have some sense of direction as to where you are headed next.

Start by getting a notepad and writing down 20 things you would like to do. If you draw a blank, don't get discouraged. Just a take a break and put the list away for a while. This is an evolving process. Think outside the box. Don't play it safe. This is a list of things you have always wanted to do. Target different areas of your life. Think about your hobbies, your relationships, your finances, your athletic ability. A majority of the items found on a bucket list usually revolve around travel. However, if you have always wanted to write a book, then definitely add that to your list, too. Read other people's lists. There are dozens of websites that give examples of bucket lists.

Refine your list. Get rid of the more impossible or improbable tasks that are likely to never happen. Don't scratch out items simple because you don't have the courage. If learning how to downhill ski is one of your goals and your just not sure if you can do this, then factor in time to take lessons to build up your confidence. Start small by making some of the things on your list easier to achieve than others. This will keep you motivated and encouraged to work toward reaching all of your goals. Be on the lookout for new ideas. While you are meeting new people every day, practice being an attentive listener when you find yourself in social settings. Quickly jot down any new ideas you hear using a note pad you can install on your phone as an App. The objective of a bucket list is to not only have fun, but to find meaning. By doing the items on your list, you are striving for fulfillment and inner growth. There are many kinds of bucket lists depending on your interests. Below I have assembled several lists organized by subject. Take a look and see if any of these suggestions ignite a curiosity. If so, add those items to your own list.

AN ADVENTURES BUCKET LIST

1. Ride in a hot air balloon.
2. Go paragliding.
3. Go parasailing in Acapulco.
4. Go sky diving.
5. Go on a helicopter ride.
6. Go scuba diving.
7. Go snorkeling in a shipwreck.
8. Swim with sharks.
9. Ride a mechanical bull.
10. Climb Mount Kilimanjaro.
11. Climb Mount Everest.
12. Go fire walking.
13. Go bungee jumping.
14. Go white water rafting.
15. Race a sports car.

ATTITUDE & PASSION

16. Break a Guinness World Record.
17. Go rock climbing.
18. Learn to fly a plane.

PLACES TO VISIT BUCKET LIST

1. Walk the Golden Gate Bridge in San Francisco
2. Go to the Pike Place Market in Seattle
3. See Mount Rushmore
4. Visit the Empire State Building
5. Walk up the Statue of Liberty
6. Visit SeaWorld Florida, Orlando
7. Go to Universal Studios, Hollywood, CA
8. Waikiki Beach, Oahu, Hawaii
9. Disney World

MUSEUMS BUCKET LIST

1. El Prado in Madrid, Spain
2. The Uffizi Gallery in Florence, Italy
3. The Hermitage in St. Petersburg, Russia

4. The Metropolitan Museum of Art in New York

5. The British Museum in London, England

6. The Van Gogh Museum, Amsterdam, Holland

7. The Egyptian Museum in Cairo

8. The Art Institute in Chicago

9. The Smithsonian Museums in Washington, DC

HOBBIES BUCKET LIST

1. Learn to fly a kite.

2. Learn how to perform magic tricks.

3. Make mobiles.

4. Keep bees.

5. Learn to juggle

6. Solve the Rubik's Cube

7. Construct furniture.

8. Do woodworking.

9. Make stained glass windows.

10. Learn to make candles.

11. Make models of cars, ships or airplanes.

ATTITUDE & PASSION

12. Building doll houses.

13. Learn to brew beer.

14. Take up gourmet cooking.

15. Learn to paint – watercolors, oil, acrylics.

16. Gardening

17. Grow prize-winning roses.

18. Restore a classic car.

CHAPTER 7
TIME

"Time is the coin of your life. It is the only coin you have, and only you can determine how it will be spent. Be careful lest you let other people spend it for you."

~ Carl Sandburg

How you spend your time is critical to creating an exceptional life. I learned the value of my time after I had children. Spending my time working in corporate America could not compare to time spent caring for my babies. I made the decision to leave my job and take five years off to raise my two sons during their formative years. It was one of the best decisions I've ever made. When I got back in the rat race of life, I still found ways to carved out "pockets of time" with each of my children, even if it was just to share an ice cream cone together. I struggled with time later on in my life. Here's what got in the way: perfectionism, control, beauty, people, and a need to be busy.

PERFECTIONISM

I've been guilty of perfectionism. I've dedicated copious amounts of time and attention to my work and my life to maintain high personal standards. My passion for excellence has driven me to go the extra mile, never relenting until I've done it right. However, what happens when we get carried away with perfectionism? We become disgruntled and discouraged, even depressed, when we fail to meet the impossibly high standards we set for ourselves, making us reluctant to take on new challenges or even finish tasks we've already started. Unfortunately, I have quit many jobs because I felt like I wasn't measuring up to meeting every expectation of the position. True perfectionists have a hard time starting things and an even harder time finishing them. What I've learned is that the real world doesn't reward perfectionists. It rewards people who get things done. Now that I've had cancer, I'm not wasting any more of my time trying to be perfect. I spending my time enjoying life!

CONTROL

Are you a control freak? I used to be and sometimes I still am. I've wasted much time and emotional energy on things that are beyond my control. I have found this to be is a recipe for frustration and misery. Some forces are just out of our control. We need to adjust our thinking. Consuming yourself with the negative aspects of a circumstance is a waste of time. However, if you look at the circumstance productively and positively, coming from the standpoint of "What's my next best move?" you put yourself back in the driver's seat. Here's what I've learned: some forces are out of my control. I've accepted this fact of life. Simply move on and spend your time doing what you enjoy.

TRANSFORMATION

BEAUTY

I've spent hundreds of hours sitting in beauty salons getting my hair cut, colored, highlighted, straightened, trimmed, and even more time getting manicures, pedicures, facials, brow waxes, lip waxes and massages. You name it, I've had it done in a salon. When I went through chemotherapy, I lost all the hair off my head, my arms, my legs, my eye brows and my eye lashes. I even lost the peach fuzz off my face. When I looked in the mirror, I realized I was down to the bare bones of beauty. That's when it dawned on me just how much time, precious time, I had wasted in beauty salons. I had also spent a lot time worrying about making sure I looked a certain way. For who? Boyfriends, husbands, friends, people I don't even know? I've learned that there is no right way to dress or wear my hair. Trying to look like someone else is a waste of my time. In this crazy world that tries to make you look like everyone else, find the courage to be yourself.

BUSYNESS

In his book, *The 4-Hour Workweek*, Tim Ferris says, "Slow down and remember this: Most things make no difference. Being busy is often a form of mental laziness – lazy thinking and indiscriminate action."[16] Busy people are rushing all over the place, and running late half of the time. They are heading to work, conferences, meetings, social engagements, etc. They barely have enough free time for family get-togethers and they rarely get enough sleep. Their busy schedule gives them an elevated sense of importance. However, it's all an illusion. They are like hamsters running on a wheel.

I have been guilty of busyness. Very guilty. I went through an obsessive phase of organizational management of the home. Some of you may know what I'm referring to. The repeated cycle of cleaning, organizing, tossing and shopping. It made feel like I had something important to do. Now I realize that I wasted much of my time organizing closets when I could have spent that time on my relationships with my family and friends. Here's my solution: Slow down. Breathe. Put first things first. Do one thing at a time. I like what Mariel Hemingway and Bobby Williams had to say about time in their book, *The WillingWay*, "Experience each moment of life more fully with vibrancy and vitality." Mariel and Bobby explain that, "Simple activities like watching a sunrise instead of sleeping in, drinking water out of glass instead of plastic, and taking time away from technology to get outside are some of the natural ways to tune into ourselves and to make far-reaching differences in our lives, our relationships, and our world."[17]

PEOPLE

Friends, family, coworkers, colleagues, even acquaintances can eat up your time, especially if they are toxic people. Toxic people drain you. They leave you feeling psychologically and emotionally depleted after spending time with them. They are unreliable. Toxic people always break their promises. They only contact you when they need something. Otherwise, you never hear from them. They are jealous of you. They want what you have and they want to take it away from you. Toxic people have zero ambition. Being around people with no ambition is a waste of your time. You constantly find yourself daydreaming about all the other things you'd rather be doing with your time besides talking with them. Can you think of a few people in your life who are toxic?

Be smart when it comes to spending your precious time with other people. In creating an exceptional life, start associating with people who are likeminded, focused, and supportive. Socialize with people who create energy when they enter the room versus those who create energy when they leave. Reach out to connected, influential individuals who are aligned with your dreams and goals. Seth Godin wrote an excellent book, *Tribes: We Need You to Lead Us*, on finding a tribe and working together to make a difference in all of our lives. We are the sum of the people we spend the most time with. If you hang with the wrong people, they will negatively affect you. However, if you hang with the right people, you will be enriching your exceptional life.

CHAPTER 8
RELATIONSHIPS

"The quality of your life is the quality of your relationships."

~ Anthony Robbins

When we think of creating an exceptional life, we have to consider the people that we spend our time with. Clearly, we have to take a look at our relationships with the closest people in our lives - our relationships with our spouse or partner, our children, our parents, friends and coworkers. In order for us to move forward into a more rewarding life, we have to first step back and acknowledge what didn't work in the past when it came to relationships. For most of us, what we really want is to find a means

GETTING HEALTHY IN RELATIONSHIPS

of navigating our way into healthy relationships and staying connected to others throughout our cancer survivorship.

When I reflect back on my past relationships, I see that at the beginning I have been on equally footing with the man from a socioeconomic and emotional standpoint. The relationship goes along fine for the first few years. However, what usually happens over time is that I begin to lose a sense of who I am in the relationship. In her book, *The Dance of Anger: A Woman's Guide to Changing the Patterns of Intimate Relationships*, Harriet Lerner, PhD explains the concept of de-selfing. She states that de-selfing "occurs when one person, often a wife, does more giving in and going along than is her share and does not have a sense of clarity about her decisions and control over her choices. De-selfing means that too much of one's self (including one's thoughts, wants, beliefs, and ambitions) is 'negotiable' under pressure from the relationship." I believe the de-selfing process can begin for a woman when she feels pressure to change her last name once she is married.

A form of de-selfing, common to women, is called 'under-functioning.' The "under-functioning over-functioning pattern is a familiar one in couples. How does it work? Like a seesaw, it is the under-functioning of one individual that allows for the over-functioning of the other. For example, the more the man avoids sharing his own weaknesses, neediness, and vulnerability, the more the woman may experience and express more than her share. The more the woman avoids showing her competence and strength, the more her man will have an inflated sense of his own."[18]

It is at this point in my relationships when I have repressed both my anger and my emotions to the point of becoming utterly depressed out of my mind. In the past, my typical pattern of behavior would have been to seek out a therapist who would inevitably put me on an antidepressant to fix the relationship. Now that I've recognized my vulnerability toward 'de-selfing' myself in relationships, I can take this new awareness with me on my journey to finding a partner who is open to a more constructive and assertive relationship in my new life post cancer.

LETTING GO OF EMOTIONAL REPRESSION

Another area that I've struggled with is emotionally repressing my feelings. For most of my life, I've stuffed my reactions to difficult problems deep inside of me by overindulging in food. The relationship between cancer and withheld emotion has been documented in numerous studies. Dr. Bernie Siegel spoke about the effect of this quiet desperation in his book, *Love, Medicine & Miracles: Lessons Learned About Self-Healing From a Surgeon's Experience with Exceptional Patients*. He writes that when "working with breast-cancer patients, Mogens Jensen of the Yale psychology department showed that defensive-repressors die faster than with patients who have a more realistic outlook. These are the smiling ones who don't acknowledge their desperation, who say, "I'm fine," even though you know they have cancer, their spouses have run off, their children are drug addicts, and the house just burned down. Jensen believed this behavior 'disregulates' and exhausts the immune system because it is confused by the mixed messages."[19]

We emotionally repress our thoughts and feelings for many reasons. We do it to keep up appearances. "What will the neighbors think if they really knew what was going on in our house?" We also do it to avoid confrontation. When our spouse or partner asks us, "What's wrong, you seem quiet?" We may avoid eye contact and switch topics to dodge having a fight. We may have held back our responses as children to avoid the repercussions of being disciplined. We may also refrain from expressing negative emotions in public because our culture has taught us to be politically correct. For this reason, we may feel ashamed or afraid of our emotions so therefore we hide them or repress them.

Dr. Siegel explains that, "Both men and women are subject to hopelessness, but because of their often divergent roles, the situations that trigger it are often different. Men are generally better able to express anger, while women tend to hold it in and become depressed." He continues by stating "to some extent, then, cancer is not a primary disease. It is partly a reaction to a set of circumstances that weaken the body's defenses." So how do we let go of our emotional repression and get healthy? Once we have identify our beliefs that are affecting our perceptions negatively, then we can begin to experience emotional freedom. I distinctly remember my life coach saying to me, "Stop worrying about what other people think of you. Just get out there and start living your life." At first, I didn't think this was possible. However, she kept reminding me that what others may think about me is none of my business. Instead, I began directing my energy into learning how to express myself authentically without the fear of being judged.

Have you ever noticed that happy people usually don't repress their feelings. They freely share what's going on in their day, either at home or work, and they don't fear being rejected. They just let it out, good or bad. Dr. Siegel writes, "The simple truth is, happy people generally don't get sick. One's attitude toward oneself is the single most important factor in healing or staying well. Those who are at peace with themselves and their immediate surroundings have far fewer serious illnesses than those who are not."[20]

EXPERIENCING JOY IN RELATIONSHIPS

Learning to be happy in my own skin and asserting myself in my relationships are two changes that I can make toward creating an exceptional life. What about the joy of loving? How can I experience joy in my relationships with other people? I have done much reading on the topic of joy mostly because I've spent so much of my life in angst. When I was diagnosed with cancer, I decided that enough time had been spent feeling sad, mad and angry. I wanted to discover how to find contentment, peace and joy in my interactions with others. I found that the key is to be present in the moment; to experience *what is*.

Susan Campbell, PhD explains in her book, *Getting Real: Ten Truth Skills You Need to Live an Authentic Life,* that "As you practice experiencing *what is*, you attain more perspective; you see from a wider vantage point. You discover that jobs, money, admirers, possessions, good moods, bad moods, lucky breaks, failures,

TRANSFORMATION

and misfortunes come and go. Experiencing *what is* helps you draw a bigger circle around the ups and downs of your existence. The ups and downs are not separate. Together they comprise your life, your hero's journey."[21] Dr. Campbell says, "The greatest gift you can give yourself and others is your free, open attention: your presence. By letting go of the need to be right, safe, and certain in favor of being real, unique, and open to surprise, you affirm yourself as a living, ever-changing presence, participating in life's changes instead of trying to control them."[22]

I began making myself available to experience *what is* in my friendships with other women. I started by interacting with others in an honest, down-to-earth manner by allowing them to drop by spontaneously to visit. Instead of screening my calls, I answered my telephone, responded to emails promptly and said, "Yes," to last minute invitations. My circle of friends grew exponentially when I started accepting opportunities to experience *what is*. Eckhart Tolle described this concept beautifully in his book, *The Power Of Now*, when he said, "As soon as you honor the present moment, all unhappiness and struggle dissolve, and life begins to flow with joy and ease. When you act out the present-moment awareness, whatever you do becomes imbued with a sense of quality, care, and love - even the most simple action."[23]

HOW TO STAY CONNECTED TO OTHERS

As a cancer survivor, there have been many times that I felt alone or different from my friends. There were times when I felt confused about the next steps in my journey or simply needed the comfort of talking with others who had successfully won their battle against cancer. I participated in a variety of cancer support groups. A few provided an atmosphere of camaraderie. The others, however, were downright depressing as if the group members were wallowing in a perpetual pool of cancer reoccurrence. The most effective way for me to stay connected to others during my cancer journey was through social media. It allowed me to keep everyone up to date with my progress. I also created and wrote a blog called *The Healing Blog: Creating An Exceptional Life*. This medium allowed me to post weekly online entries, along with photo images of my diagnosis, treatment, discoveries and lessons learned on my journey through cancer. The beauty of writing a blog is that it gives your readers an opportunity to respond to your entries by leaving their comments. Below is an expanded description of how to use social media, blogs and the Internet to stay connected to others:

<u>Social Media</u>

Social media is a place to stay in touch. Creating a network of friends and family you can reach out to will allow you to share and reap the wisdom of others who are on the same path. There are **Facebook Pages** of organizations to join that offer information on a regular basis like: American Cancer Society, The Breast Cancer Site Store, Click a day for Breast Cancer, Survivor Breast Cancer, and many more.

There are also many **Group Pages** you can join on Facebook: Cancer Support Group, CanSupport - Caring for People with Cancer, etc. To find groups type into the search box "find all pages" then add cancer and your city or state or type of cancer and find a group to join. For example: *"Breast cancer groups in New Mexico."* You can join in the conversations and make a few friends.

Other sites also offer great information and support. **Pinterest.com** has hundreds of boards dedicated to Cancer – Cancer Quotes, Living with Cancer, Cancer Stinks, Cancer Survivors, Cancer Blogs and many more; each with a plethora of resources and inspiration.

Blogs

Writing a cancer blog is a way for you to find out how others are coping with the uncertainty of cancer –what they do to keep their spirits high and information on what is working for them. Just Goggle "cancer blogs 2013" and you will find an abundance of blogs to choose from. You may just catch the "Blogging Bug" yourself and add your voice to the conversation.

TRANSFORMATION

The Internet

Caution: Don't take as gospel everything you read online. There are trusted sites online that you will find useful such as **epocrates.com**. Keeping track of your medications can get tricky. Patients and families may have difficulty when one medication can be used for different needs or when they have more than one pill for the same problem.

Another trusted online source is **mayoclinic.com**. Here you can research almost anything and be confident that the information is current and accurate. Under the tab *Health Information* you can find symptom checker, drugs and supplements, tests and procedures, healthy living, and expert blogs.

~ Barbara Lemaire, PhD
Social Media Made Simple

CHAPTER 9
FEAR

"You gain strength, courage and confidence by every experience in which you really stop to look fear in the face."

~ Eleanor Roosevelt

This chapter on fear was clearly the most difficult one for me to write. I procrastinated over and over, deciding whether to included it in my book. Obviously, I had a very big fear of writing this chapter because in doing so it would forced me to deal with my own fears out loud. After attending my son's college graduation, followed by my niece's high school graduation and then seeing my family for the first time since my cancer diagnosis, all my fears suddenly collided at once resulting in a watershed of tears. I cried continuously for three days straight and couldn't seem to find the courage or strength to get a grip. It was clearly time for me to write about fear.

Being told you have cancer is scary. It's HUGE scary. It makes you want to open the front door of your home and scream, "HELP!" at the loudest decibels you can muster up. It conjures up every imaginable fear you could possibly think of. It can feel so BIG in your brain that you don't know how to process it. It is so much bigger than a turbulent plane flight, facing a criminal in a dark alley, or losing your job. This is your life! Now your whole life is in jeopardy. Somehow, someway, you got a free lifetime membership into the "Cancer Club." Now you are looking for every avenue you can find to cancel your membership and get the hell out of this awful club.

OF DEATH AND DYING

I never spent much time thinking about my own death. Sure, I'd been to funerals and experienced other peoples deaths.

FEAR

However, I was simply too busy raising children, working, and being married to acknowledge that one day this crazy roller coaster ride of a life would come to a screeching halt. Then, at age 51, I received a cancer diagnosis. It was a wake up call on so many levels. It erupted a terrifying fear deep inside of me - the fear of dying.

I had battled with fear previously in my life such as the fear of flying and the fear of losing my children. The fear of dying was too huge for me to digest. I couldn't wrap my head around the idea of not being there for my children or possibly not living long enough to enjoy my grandchildren. I was distraught with this awful fear but didn't know where to turn to for help. How could I bring up the topic of death with my friends who were living every minute of their life with complete gusto? Did my family really want to hear about my fear of death or would it just sound like me whining and feeling sorry for myself?

Dr. David Servan-Schreiber did a beautiful job of describing the process of dying in his international bestselling book,

TRANSFORMATION

Anticancer: A New Way of Life. In his chapter on Defusing Fear, Dr. Servan-Schreiber writes,

> "With relief we found out that death isn't painful in itself. In the final days, the dying no longer feel like eating or drinking. The body dehydrates progressively. No more secretions, no more urine or stools, less phlegm in the lungs. Thus less pain in the abdomen, less nausea. There is no more vomiting, no more coughing. The whole body slows down. The mouth is often dry, but it's easy to relieve the dryness by sucking on small ice cubes with a feeling of well-being, sometimes even mild euphoria. The dying are less interested in talking, simply holding a hand or looking through the window at the sunlight or listening to birdsong or particularly beautiful music instead. In the final hours, one sometimes hears a different kind of breathing called the "death rattle." And then there are several final incomplete breaths (the "last breath") and

involuntary contractions of the body and face, which seem to be resisting the loss of the life force. These do not betray suffering but are simply a sign of the lack of oxygen in the tissues. Then the muscles let go and everything is over."[24]

After reading this section on the process of dying, I suddenly felt a wave of peace sweep over me. It felt like a beautiful, relaxing way to take my last breaths of life while being surrounded by my family. When my time comes, I want to pass into my next life with a peaceful good bye to all my love ones.

OF CANCER REOCCURRENCE

There isn't a cancer survivor anywhere that doesn't carry the fear of their cancer returning. Every ache or pain or sudden dizzy spell causes one to ponder the question, "Is my cancer back?" Sounds like an awful way to live, right? Well, I began to experience this fear for the first time right after my chemotherapy was completed. There was a short time between the end of my chemo and the start of my radiation therapy when I felt afraid of my cancer coming back. I began to regret not having had a mastectomy. My tumor was small and my breast surgeon reassured me that a lumpectomy was appropriate, followed by chemotherapy and radiation. However, I became fearful that I hadn't taken extreme enough measures to remove all my breast tissue so therefore, quite possibly, my cancer could return. This fear was followed by the fear of radiation therapy. I was afraid of my skin being permanently burned. I was also afraid of damage to my heart muscle from the radiation beam since my breast cancer was located in my left breast.

Sometimes my fear of reoccurrence would become so large in my head that it would interfere with eating and sleeping. There were many times when I would be over wrought with the fear that sugar feeds cancer cells. This in turn would cause my body to literally shut down at the sight of dessert, snacks, fancy coffee drinks, alcohol, candy or gum. Sounds like a good way to lose weight, right? Not really. When avoiding sugar becomes an obsessive fear, than it really becomes more of a daily battle not a weight loss program. Sometimes I would lie awake at night thinking about my cancer, asking myself over and over, "Have I done everything I can to remove my cancer and increase my chances of survival?" We all want peace inside from this insidious fear but really what it comes down to is faith.

OF LIVING LIFE EXCEPTIONALLY WELL

As a woman, I know deep inside that I have held myself back from really living and experiencing life. Part of it comes from what was modeled to me as a child. Although my father clearly impressed upon me the importance of a college education, it was my mother's role of wife and mother that I identified with the most. My mother made a life for herself in the home where she appeared to be content and happy.

After I graduated from college, I wasn't really interested in starting a career. I wanted a baby. I wanted to start my life as a mother. Instead, I waited five years while my husband at the time established his career. In the meantime, I worked various jobs,

TRANSFORMATION

mostly dead end jobs, to keep myself busy until we were ready to start a family. Right now as I write this I can feel the heat running down the back of my neck as feminists far and wide are probably rolling their eyes reading about my old fashioned outlook on life after college.

Even after I had children and went back to work to establish a successful teaching career, I was still more interested and fulfilled by my work as a mother. I was not a risk-taker by nature. I was a "safety-girl" and I liked to do things by the book. There was safety and security in being a conservative wife and mother and following the rules. As a young woman and a mother, I prided myself on being "nice," on being approved of, and going along at the sacrifice of truly developing my own ideas, dreams and exceptional life. To be honest, I really had no idea that their could be a life outside this traditional box. The other part of it is that I was scared to strike out on my own. I was afraid of failing. I was afraid of getting lost. I was afraid of getting hurt along the way. I was afraid of really living my life for all that it could be.

FEAR

My adult life, up to the age of 50, had been spent in an anxious state of fear about one thing or another. I now realize that to live in fear is to build a cage around ourselves. Trapped by our own fears, we shut ourselves down and become content with living a small life. We feel that by limiting our exposure to others and diminishing our life experiences, that we will be freed from our anxiety and that joy will be waiting for us in the end. This is not the case, of course. To really conquer our fears, we must master the courage to have our own power and to live our life exceptionally well.

In my search to be engaged and to live fully alive, I found an author who truly sums up fearlessness. Arianna Huffington bravely wrote in her book, *On Becoming Fearless in Love, Work, and Life*, what living the fearless life is really about:

> "When we know who we are, we can overcome our fears and insecurities. We surpass our smaller selves who suffer the slings and arrows of our conditioned reality, and we move to the unconditional truth of our larger

selves. The answers to the questions of what to say, what to do, whom to let in, and whom to keep out become a clear and simple matter of listening to our hearts. That inner voice helps us align with our purpose, because each of us has a purpose, even if we judge it to be insignificant. The voice is there. We just need to listen to it. When we do that, we live in fearlessness."[25]

Thank you, Arianna, for inspiring me to live my life fearlessly.

CHAPTER 10
SPIRITUALITY

"Spiritual relationship is far more precious than physical. Physical relationship divorced from spiritual is body without soul."

~ **Mahatma Gandhi**

MY SPIRITUAL JOURNEY

Spirituality is something I have explored most of my life. I was born and raised a Catholic, participating in the essential sacraments of this religion: baptism, holy communion, confirmation and confession. When I went away to college, I explore Christianity and began attending the Vineyard Church. Later on, while working full time and living in Hawaii, I don't remember

TRANSFORMATION

attending any one church specifically. When I returned to the mainland and started a family, I found the Catholic church to be cold and robotic. My neighbor at the time suggested the local Lutheran church and highly recommended its preschool for my children. So began my journey attending St. Paul's Lutheran church which was a welcoming congregation and a mainstay during my children's formative years. Unfortunately, after seven years this local Lutheran church changed its rules and would only allow orthodox Lutherans to attend.

I returned to the Christian church for another seven years until my husband's career transferred us to the East Coast. Here, I became fascinated with the Washington National Cathedral and attended Episcopalian church services for three years. I loved the formality of this church and appreciated receiving weekly communion again. Later on, while I was transitioning through a divorce, I friend invited me to attend a weekly bible study with the Jehovah's Witnesses, which I did for 18 months, but I soon realized that my Christian faith could not be changed.

SPIRITUALITY

When I returned to New Mexico, I found a local church in the mountains that immediately opened their doors to me. At this church, I developed trusted friendships with others through the Women's ministry which led to monthly social outings and holiday get togethers. The Caring For Others ministry was my lifeline during cancer treatments as many church members volunteered to drive me to chemotherapy, accompany me to doctor appointments, and assist me with household chores. My path to finding spirituality has been a curious journey of exploration. I have always been fascinated with religions around the globe and respect each individual's right to choose a spiritual path without discrimination or prejudice.

DAILY AFFIRMATIONS AND DEVOTIONS

While I was going through chemotherapy, I found myself deeply saddened and, at times, profoundly depressed. I had always had my faith in God to guide me through most of life's ups and downs, but cancer was totally different from anything I'd been through before. There were many times during my chemotherapy

TRANSFORMATION

treatments that I was simply too nauseous to attend weekly church service. Instead, I often found myself lying on the living couch while staring at the ceiling and contemplating the meaning of life. Two books got me through this difficult phase of my recovery: *The Joy of Loving: A guide to daily living with Mother Theresa* and *Jesus Calling: Enjoying peace in His presence* by Sarah Young.

The Joy of Loving consists of messages written by Mother Teresa and compiled by Jaya Chalika and Edward Le Joly. This guide for daily spiritual living includes messages for each calendar day and is useful to both the believer and the nonbeliever. The authors write, "Mother Teresa speaks as the conscience of the world. She is a lighthouse for believers, sending rays of light that show the way in semi-darkness. And to nonbelievers in God, she is an anchor steadying their ship in rough waters."[26] Each morning over breakfast, I look forward to opening this book and reading an inspirational message from Mother Teresa to start my day.

In *Jesus Calling*, Young writes devotions for every day of the calendar year, including scriptural references after each reading. Her book includes themes of thankfulness and trust recurring throughout which she states are essential to experiencing peace with our higher power. Both thought-provoking and instructional, *Jesus Calling* teaches us the practice of listening to God. Young writes,

> "A life-changing verse has been 'Be still, and know that I am God' (Psalm 46:10). Alternate readings for 'Be still' are 'Relax,' 'Let go,' and 'Cease striving' (NASB). This is an enticing invitation from God to lay down our cares and seek His Presence. I believe that God yearns for these quiet moments with us even more than we do. I also believe that He still speaks to those who listen to Him (John 10:27), and I continually depend on the Holy Spirit's help in this."[27]

Every day for six weeks, I commuted 25 minutes each way to receive my daily dose of radiation therapy at the cancer center. I was only under the radiation beam for five minutes which hardly justified all the driving back and forth. However, it was the daily devotions in the pocket book, *Jesus Calling*, which kept my mind peaceful and calm throughout my treatment. In addition, I downloaded an App called *Unique Daily Affirmations*. I read and reread my affirmation throughout the day which inspired me to continue on my path to positive living.

THE SPIRITUAL SIDE OF AN EXCEPTIONAL LIFE

Recovering and surviving from cancer can be a time of confusion and uncertainty when every suppressed emotion rises up to tear us down. Choosing to include a spiritual side to your exceptional life may feel overwhelming, but at the same time we know that a spiritual life is a worthwhile choice. We may wonder about the practicality of it. How can we live spiritually when everything around us is based on the material world?

Although personal and spiritual growth comes from within, most people appreciate the friendship, support and companionship of belonging to a religious affiliation or spiritual center. Through a spiritual relationship with a higher power, you will feel good about yourself and discover the peace and joy of abundant living. Spirituality can provide you with a foundation to go back to no matter what happens in your life. Furthermore, the power of prayer helps us experience a stronger connection with God every day. During my first year of survival, I met another cancer survivor whose faith and abounding joy stood out among all the others in our support group. Below is Jo Anne's story of how she wrestled with a diagnosis of cancer and allowed her faith to guide her through the battle.

PERSEVERANCE

By Jo Anne Parish

On a road trip to the ocean to spend a week with my sweet husband by my side, a couple of our kids sleeping in the back seat, the others following close behind in another car. I remember the moment so clearly. I was kicking back in my seat, eyes closed, listening to great tunes. The windows were open and a gentle breeze was blowing through my hair. I could almost smell the clean

TRANSFORMATION

crisp ocean air that was just a few short hours away. I always love these gatherings, I thought to myself, imagining the smiles on everyone's faces, the tight hugs I would receive…..my family is such a blessing! Suddenly, my delight was interrupted by the phone call that would changed my life forever. Within a few short seconds of my "hello," the bad news was confirmed through the harsh message, "I received the results from pathology and I'm sorry to tell you, it's cancer." I couldn't breathe, I couldn't swallow, tears poured out of my eyes. I was desperate to run, desperate to hide but there was no escape from the brutal reality… I have cancer.

What I endured the following nine months was something I could have never imagined, nor prepared for. The day after my second surgery, I received an offer for a job that was a promotional opportunity. Not only was I faced with the decision of whether to accept this new position, but whether to accept it knowing that my cancer had

SPIRITUALITY

recently been upgraded from stage 2 to stage 3. After a lengthy discussion with my new employer, I accepted the position and started the Monday after my first chemotherapy treatment. Knowing that I was a cancer patient, I was concerned that my employer and coworkers would be skeptical and watchful of me requiring "special treatment" or excessive time off, so I made sure to do neither. The first 12 weeks of chemo did not agree with me and I experienced many days where I was very, very sick.

Often, I would use my lunch break as a time to go out to my car and "rest" for the half hour. My car lent a peaceful space, away from others, and I kept a pillow there for extra comfort. One day the nausea was particularly hard and when I got into my car, I grabbed my pillow and doubled over in agony. It was the first time I really questioned whether I could continue. I was facing defeat and prepared to surrender. Somehow, I had managed to keep a smile pasted on my face, best I could, until now.

TRANSFORMATION

Deep inside I had crumbled and was broken. I cried out to God "help me," begging Him to make me strong again, to get me through this battle.

The next morning I was disappointed to discover the gloom that had so tightly embraced me the night before continued its stronghold. I dragged myself out of bed and over to brush my teeth and get ready for the day. A quick glance in the mirror forced me to take a second look; a deeper concentrated look. Who the heck was that person looking back at me? My eyes were empty….no joy, no life, no fight. I no longer knew this person standing before me. What on earth was I doing? Submitting to this illness, because it said so? I had a long haul in front of me……I couldn't continue like this. It was that moment that forced me to dig deep, beyond the diagnosis, beyond the side effects of the treatment, beyond my weariness, beyond defeat and land in my core. It was time to redirect my focus to the positive things that were present in

SPIRITUALITY

my life and practice gratefulness. Every morning, on my daily commute, I began identifying five things I felt grateful for and how much they each meant to me. Before I knew it I found myself looking forward to getting on the freeway and spouting off the many blessings I was experiencing. Acknowledging the meaningfulness of each blessing solidified my appreciation.

What was once devastation had been replaced with hope, love and faith. The greatest thing of all is that Joy found its way back into my heart! There is a lot to be said about gratefulness......it certainly is contagious. Often people marvel at the fact that I continued to work full time through the surgeries and treatments, but I never recognized that as a accomplishment. If anything, work was a true gift to me, a distraction leaving me little time to dwell on the real stuff.....the guts and the grind of the battle! Wherever we are in our lives, whatever hand we are dealt, we somehow muster up enough within to do what we have to do to wake up the next morning. When the next morning arrives, we do it all over again.

FOUNDATIONS FOR SPIRITUAL LIVING

As you begin to create your new life post cancer, consider building a foundation for your spiritual self. Be mindful of what you are doing and of where you put your attention. Mindfulness helps us stay connected to our priorities. What brings us peace and joy is the foundation of our inner priorities: being spiritual lead, speaking our truth, and loving kindness. You will find that your inner priorities are more important than your outer priorities. Treat yourself with compassion when you fall down on your priorities. Below are five basic principles that guide my spiritual self:

1. We are spiritual beings created in God's image. The God is the source and creator of all. There is no other enduring power. God is good and present everywhere.
2. The spirit of God lives within each person; therefore, all people are inherently good.

SPIRITUALITY

3. We create our life experiences through our way of thinking.
4. There is power in affirmative prayer, which we believe increases our connection with God.
5. Knowledge of these spiritual principles is not enough. We must live them.[28]

In addition, consider meeting with the pastor or the spiritual leader of your local church if you have questions about how to proceed with your spiritual journey. There are many ministry groups, retreats and bible studies in your local community that can offer you the opportunity to make caring friendships with like-minded individuals. Another avenue for developing your spiritual self is through broadcasts and podcasts. James MacDonald, the founder of Harvest Bible Chapel, developed a bible-teaching broadcast ministry, Walk in the Word, in 1997. His ministry, which now reaches 3 million people, can be easily followed by audio and video broadcasts and podcasts. You can also develop yourself spiritually through books, music, blogs, apps and

TRANSFORMATION

tours of your favorite spiritual leader. Let your curiosity lead you on your spiritual path. Reach out and connect with others as you explore your spiritual self.

CONCLUSION

"I don't think of all the misery but of the beauty that still remains."

~ **Anne Frank**

Many cancer survivors will say they are thankful for having cancer because it taught them so many lessons and made them better people. They have used their diagnosis to minister to others or to improve their community. Other survivors have responded that having cancer has helped them become more focused on priorities, with a deeper sense of purpose in life. My journey through cancer has been transformational on every level: physically, emotionally, and spiritually. I've made some dramatic lifestyle changes. Gone are sweet deserts, cookie snacks, ice cream, and anything with sugar. Now, I enjoy a daily 'green drink' made from an assortment of delicious fruits and vegetables. There's a lot less television watching as I've replaced this sedentary activity with working out at the gym four times a week. I've also learned the value of each day. Life is precious and sweet. I no longer dwell on the little things, or even the big things for that matter. The hassle and turmoil are no longer worth it.

Cancer can change your perspective on everything. I see people differently now. I'm more of an attentive listener. When I find myself interacting with someone who still smokes, drinks heavily or is obese, I want to hold their hand and share with them my journey to healthy living. Unlike people who've never had cancer, I know just how fragile the human body is and just how close death lives. This is an enormous emotional burden to carry. However, there is life after cancer. I do know what hope is and I've learned that hope is something cancer can never take from me. I'm so thankful for the second chance to live life passionately and fully. Creating an exceptional life is about taking a moment

CONCLUSION

to reflect on your life and then exploring what truly excites you. It's about using your time wisely and going after all that life has to offer you.

SURVIVORSHIP

Cancer is life altering. Once treatment is over, cancer survivors deal with their new life in different ways. Some may feel isolation and fear and wonder, "What am I going to do with the rest of my life?" As Dr. Susan Love stated so poignantly in her book, "Doctors can treat you and sometimes cure you, but *you* are in charge of your healing. The experience of having cancer will change you forever. The trick is to use it to improve your life."[29]

Survivorship is key to creating your exceptional life. It begins the day you are diagnosed with cancer. It includes everything you are doing to keep yourself alive or to put your cancer in remission: surgery, clinical trials, chemotherapy, radiation therapy, physical therapy, alternative or complementary medicine, a healthy diet and a regular exercise program. In her book, *Happiness in a Storm: Facing Illness and Embracing Life as a Healthy Survivor*, Dr.

Wendy Schlessel Harpham reminds us that, "It's important that you take an active role in your survivorship by keeping your follow up appointments, getting your periodic scans done and staying abreast of current advances in cancer research. In the same way that you participated in your initial treatment and cure, you must do diligence in the years to come if survival is your goal."[30] Take ownership of your survivorship and become the role model to those that will follow behind you in the fight against cancer.

CREATING YOUR OWN EXCEPTIONAL LIFE

My primary reason for writing this book was to reach out to others and to inspire them to celebrate their life. For those of you who have spent your life being a caregiver to others, its time for you to put your needs, desires and wants first. How will you create your own exceptional life? Now is your chance to live the life you've always dreamed of but were too scared to try. Cancer has made you stronger and wiser. You clearly know now the value of your time, your relationships, and your health. Dr. Harpham says, "Healthy survivorship is determined by *how* you live. Health

CONCLUSION

implies a wholeness of body, mind, and spirit."[31] To live an exceptional life means that *you* are in charge of your body, your mind and your spirit. It involves taking responsibility for planning your life's direction, researching your options, calculating your risks and bravely taking chances.

Throughout this book, I've shared with you the obstacles I've come across that have either stalled me, prevented me or otherwise sidetracked me from living an exceptional life. Indecision, perfectionism, fear, laziness, even busyness have been my culprits. Over and over, I hear people complain about doing activities they hate to do. They continue to fill up their weekly calendar with dreadful trips to visit their relatives, emotionally draining support groups, time consuming home renovations, and taking in more annoying pets to care for. If you hate doing something, then stop doing it. Complaining about your life will not make it better. You must take control of your life and steer it in the direction you want to go. Be determined and stay discipline in everything you do. Remember you are the driver of your life's destiny.

TRANSFORMATION

HERE ARE PRACTICAL STEPS TO CONSIDER IN CREATING YOUR NEW LIFE:

- Start by establishing a daily schedule, with an emphasis on daily exercise and healthy eating.
- Learn to express your emotions and thoughts in a healthy and authentic way.
- Practice time management.
- Assess your passions and write a bucket list.
- Create a one year, five year and ten year life plan.
- Plan your steps for reaching your goals.
- Pay attention and remember that your actions have consequences.
- Continue to get ongoing support from mentors, peers, and trusted professionals.
- Celebrate your successes along the way.

Finally, take advantage of every opportunity that comes your way to improve your life and to bring you closer to the exceptional life you deserve to live.

APPENDIX I: 10 TIPS TO FEEL EXCEPTIONAL DURING CANCER TREATMENT

The following tips supplement Chapter 2 on Cancer Treatments. I created this list of tips based on what made me feel better physically and what elevated my attitude positively during my own experience with chemotherapy and radiation therapy.

Chemo Buddies - Make a list of friends, neighbors and family members who are available to drive you and spend time with you during your chemo infusions. Rotate the people on the list so you have a different person taken you each time. Make sure you have an alternate available if your primary person has to cancel at the last minute. Plan a picnic. Ask your chemo buddy to bring a lunch, blanket, magazines and a favorite book to share. Your time at the infusion center will fly by if you have a trusted friend to share the experience with.

Caring Environment - You are going to need a listening ear and many hugs during your treatments. So surround yourself with a circle of caring, loving friends who understand the journey you are on. Where you receive your treatments is important, too. Find a cancer center with healthcare professionals who have created a homey environment of love, understanding, and gentle care.

Take a Virtual Trip - While you're going through countless CT scans, MRIs and PET scans, close your eyes and pretend you're on a trip. It can be hard to lie still for 30 to 60 minutes while you're having scans done. Close your eyes and allow yourself to drift away to an imaginary island where you can create your best ever vacation, complete with drinks, chaise lounge chairs, a gentle breeze and the sand and surf nearby.

Say "Yes" to Meals - When friends and family offer to bring you a meal, don't hesitate to say, "Yes." Be specific about what you like to eat because chemotherapy will change your tastebuds. Take this opportunity to allow others to cook and serve you when you're feeling tired and lousy. Besides, you'll enjoy the company of a friend stopping by with a home cooked meal.

Spread Encouragement - During your chemotherapy or radiation treatments, take a moment to chat with the other patients who look like they need a friend. Introduce yourself and listen to them. Hold their hand and offer a word or two of encouragement. When we reach out to others, it helps us ease out of our own depressed thoughts.

Use Your Sense of Humor - While your losing your hair, eye lashes and eye brows during chemotherapy treatments, you just have to give into it at some point. There is no need to hide under wigs and painted eye brows all the time. Surprise everyone during a dinner party by pulling off your wig and dancing carefree in the middle of the room. This will put a smile of their faces and give everyone a good laugh.

Monthly Massages - Treat yourself to a monthly healing massage while you are going through chemotherapy. The benefit of regular massage therapy will ease your bone pain, take your mind off of your treatments, and restore balance to your well being. Scrimp and save by saying, "No" to other items in your budget. By the end of the month, you'll have enough money saved to enjoy this monthly ritual.

Save Your Receipts - For medical copays, deductibles, out-of-pocket expenses, insurance premiums and prescription copays. Keep a log of all the miles you put on your car traveling to and from appointments. These expenses add up quickly. At the end of the year, your receipts and mileage may be a tax deduction on your income tax return.

A Positive Attitude - There may be times when you feel sad and discouraged during your cancer journey. Work on keeping a positive attitude by reading daily affirmations each morning when you rise. Carry a spiritual book in your purse or download an affirmations App for your phone that you can refer to when you feel yourself backsliding.

Stay Connected - Receiving a cancer diagnosis may make you want to stay home and wallow on the couch. This is self pity.

10 TIPS TO FEEL EXCEPTIONAL

Remember to stay connected to the world during your cancer treatments. You can do this through social media, writing a blog or joining a support group. Reaching out to find friends will make you feel better about your current situation.

APPENDIX II:
RESOURCE GUIDE

BOOKS

Campbell, Harriet, Ph.D. <u>Getting Real: 10 Truth Skills You Need to Live an Authentic Life</u>, (An HJ Kramer Book, published in a joint venture with New World Library, 2001). This book provides a set of profound awareness practices that support living a life of radical aliveness that comes from letting go of our attachment to being "right, safe, and certain."

Chozen Bays, Jan, M.D. <u>Mindful Eating: A Guide to Rediscovering a Healthy and Joyful Relationship with Food</u>, (Boston, MA:

Shambhala Publications, Inc., 2009). This book offers a new way to "reprogram" the way we think about and consume our food.

Hemingway, Mariel and Bobby Williams. *The WillingWay: 10 Dynamic Steps for Connecting with Nature and Revealing Your Authentic Self,* (Changing Lives Press/Never Sink Books, 2013). This book is about reconnecting to nature one step at a time to discover a more fulfilling life of simplicity, adventure, stillness, and laughter.

Huffington, Arianna. *On Becoming Fearless... in Love, Work, and Life,* (New York, NY: Little, Brown & Company, 2006). The author draws on her own experiences, and those of other women, to illustrate how to be bold from the inside out. How conquering fear is crucial to living a full life and to making a difference in the world.

Lerner, Harriet, Ph.D. *The Dance of Anger: A Woman's Guide to Changing the Patterns of Intimate Relationships*, (New York, NY: Harper Perennial, a division of HarperCollins Publishers, 1985).

RESOURCE GUIDE

Dr. Lerner teaches women to identify the true sources of our anger and to use anger as a powerful vehicle for creating meaningful and lasting change.

Love, S.M., M.D., & Lindsey, Karen. *Dr. Susan Love's Breast Book*, (Cambridge, MA: Da Capo Press, A Member of the Perseus Book Group, 2005). The standard reference book revised to reflect every new development in breast care, screening, diagnosis, treatment, and research.

Manheim, Jason. *The Healthy Green Drink Diet: Advice and Recipes to Energize, Alkalize, Lose Weight, and Feel Great*, (New York, NY: Skyhorse Publishing, 2012). The founder of heathygreendrink.com offers a persuasive argument for adding a green drink to your daily routine, as well as recipes for dozens of different variations.

Schlessel Harpham, Wendy, M.D. *Happiness in a Storm: Facing Illness and Embracing Life as a Healthy Survivor*, (New York, NY: W.W. Norton & Company, Inc., 2005). The author encourages people dealing with cancer, heart disease, diabetes, or any prolonged illness to simultaneously do all they can to overcome disease and live life to the fullest.

Schoffro Cook, Michelle, *The Ultimate pH Solution: Balance Your Body Chemistry to Prevent Disease and Lose Weight*, (New York, NY: HarperCollins Publisher, 2008). This book demonstrates how to control the level of acid in the body and reclaim ones health with a simple, step-by-step program.

Servan-Schreiber, David, M.D., Ph.D. *Anticancer: A New Way of Life*, (New York, NY: Viking Penguin, a member of Penguin Group (USA) Inc., 2008). This book addresses current developments in cancer research and offers tips on how people living with cancer can fight it and how healthy people can prevent it.

Siegel, Bernie, M.D. *Love, Medicine & Miracles: Lessons Learned About Self-healing from a Surgeon's Experience with Exceptional*

Patients, (New York, NY: Harper & Row, Publishers, Inc., 1986). This book demonstrates how miracles happen to exceptional patients every day - patients who have the courage to love.

ORGANIZATIONS FOR BREAST CANCER

National Breast Cancer Foundation

http://www.nbcf.org.au/Donate.aspx

Early detection education; Free breast care services to hospitals through the National Mammography Program.

Dr. Susan Love Research Foundation - Act With Love

http://dslrf.org/actwithlove/

Fundraising and innovative research to eradicate breast cancer forever and improve the quality of women's health.

Susan G. Komen Foundation

http://ww5.komen.org/

Funds breast cancer research, community health outreach, advocacy and programs in more than 50 countries.

The Breast Cancer Research Foundation

http://www.bcrfcure.org/

Provides funding for innovative clinical research at medical centers worldwide and increasing public awareness about good breast health.

ORGANIZATIONS FOR ALL OTHER CANCERS

AARP The Magazine: Living Through Cancer

http://www.aarp.org/health/conditions-treatments/living_through_cancer/

Information and services for seniors and cancer patients

American Cancer Society

http://www.cancer.org/

Cancer information and resources; local service locator

Good Wishes

http://www.goodwishesscarves.org/

Provides scarves for patients who experience hair loss due to cancer treatments.

RESOURCE GUIDE

Look Good... Feel Better, Helping Women With Cancer

http://lookgoodfeelbetter.org/

Provides complimentary beauty sessions to improve the self esteem and quality of life of women undergoing treatment for cancer.

National Cancer Institute

www.cancer.org

Provides data for both doctors and patients; lists clinical trials; good resource for accurate, unbiased information.

People Living Through Cancer

http://www.pltc.org/

Individual and group support programs, helping people face the challenges of cancer and improve quality of life.

Prevent Cancer Foundation

http://preventcancer.org/

TRANSFORMATION

Advocates the prevention and early detection of cancer through research, education and community outreach.

R.A. Bloch Cancer Foundation

http://www.blochcancer.org/resources/big-list-of-cancer-resources/

Powerful resource of websites for every type of cancer.

Relay for Life - American Cancer Society

http://www.relayforlife.org/

Fundraising events that help communities across the globe fight back against cancer.

Stand Up To Cancer

http://www.standup2cancer.org/

Raises funds to accelerate the pace of groundbreaking cancer research.

World Cancer Day

RESOURCE GUIDE

http://www.worldcancerday.org/

Marked on February 4 to raise awareness of cancer and to encourage its prevention, detection, and treatments - the goals of the World Cancer Declaration written in 2008.

NOTES

1. Marianne Williamson, *A Return to Love: Reflection on the Principles of "A Course in Miracles,"* Ch 7, Section 3, (New York, NY: HarperOne, an imprint of HarperCollins Publishers, 1992).
2. Elisabeth Kübler-Ross, *On Death and Dying: What the Dying Have to Teach Doctors, Nurses, Clergy, and Their Own Families,* (New York, NY: Simon & Schuster: A Touchstone Book, 1969).
3. Bernie Siegel, M.D., *Love, Medicine & Miracles: Lessons Learned About Self-healing from a Surgeon's Experience with Exceptional Patients,* (New York, NY: Harper & Row, Publishers, Inc., 1986).
4. Jan Chozen Bays, M.D., *Mindful Eating: A Guide to Rediscovering a Healthy and Joyful Relationship with Food,* (Boston, MA: Shambhala Publications, Inc., 2009), page 3.

5. Nicholas Perricone, M.D., *"Dr. Perricone's 10 Super-foods You Should Add to Your Diet Today,"* http://www.oprah.com/health/Dr-Perricones-10-Superfoods, (accessed July 17, 2013).
6. Jason Manheim, *The Healthy Green Drink Diet: Advice and Recipes to Energize, Alkalize, Lose Weight, and Feel Great*, (New York, NY: Skyhorse Publishing, 2012), pages 56-57.
7. Claire Ragozzino, *"Acid vs. Alkaline: The Science Behind Balancing Your pH"*, Vidya: Health, Culture, Food, Clarity, http://vidyacleanse.com/2013/03/acid-vs-alkaline-the-science-behind-balancing-your-ph/, (accessed October 22, 2013).
8. Jacquie Robertson, *"Sugar Is Evil and Here's Why: 7 Reasons to Banish Sugar From Your Life,"* http://jacquierobertson.wordpress.com/2013/02/06/sugar-is-evil-and-heres-why-7-reason-to-banish-sugar-from-your-life/, February 6, 2013, (accessed August 1, 2013).
9. Stevia Smart, *FAQ*, http://www.stevismart.com/faq.html, (accessed April 9, 2013).
10. *"Pumpkins - Fun Facts, Cooking & Nutrition"*, ebay, *http://www.ebay.com/gds/PUMPKINS-FUN-FACTS-COOKING-NUTRITION-/10000000001226037/g.html (accessed October 10, 2013).*
11. Chris Kessler, *"Liver: Nature's Most Potent Superfood,"* Chris Kresser L. AC, *http://chriskresser.com/natures-most-potent-superfood*, April 11, 2008, (accessed July 8, 2013).

NOTES

12. American Cancer Society, *"What Are Complementary and Alternative Methods?,"* Guide to Complementary and Alternative Cancer Methods, http://www.cancer.org/treatment/treatmentsandsideeffects/complementaryandalternativemedicine/guidelines-for-using-complementary-and-alternative-methods, (accessed July 20, 2013).

13. Efram Korngold and Harriet Beinfeld, *Between Heaven and Earth: A Guide To Chinese Medicine,* (New York, NY: A Ballentine Book, published by The Random House Publishing Group, 1991).

14. This work was supported through National Cancer Institute grants R21CA108084, U19CA121503 and CA016672. The authors have no conflicts of interest to report. In addition to Cohen, MD Anderson authors on the paper include: Zhongxing Liao, M.D., Department of Radiation Oncology; Qi Wei, Integrative Medicine Program and Kathryn Milbury, Ph.D., Department of Behavioral Science. Other authors include Zhen Chen, M.D., Jiayi Chen, M.D., Zhiqiang Meng, M.D., Ph.D., Wenying Bei, M.D., Ying Zhang, Xiaoma Guo, Luming Liu, M.D., Ph.D., all of Fudan University Cancer Hospital; Jennifer McQuade, M.D., Hospital of the University of Pennsylvania; Clemens Kirschbaum, Ph.D., Dresden University of Technology; and Bob Thornton, Merck & Co., Inc (on MD Anderson staff when research was conducted).

15. Talea Miller, *"In Many Countries, Cancer Patients Face Stigma, Misperceptions: A growing body of research looks at perceptions of cancer and the stigma for patients, both self-inflicted and from their communities,"* PBS News hour, http://www.pbs.org/newshour/updates/health/jan-june11/cancerstigma_06-15.htm, (accessed August 2, 2013).
16. Timothy Ferris, *The 4-Hour Workweek: Escape 9-5, Live Anywhere, and Join the New Rich,* (New York, NY: Crown Publishers, an imprint of the Crown Publishing Group, a division of Random House, Inc., 2007).
17. Mariel Hemingway and Bobby Williams, *The WillingWay: 10 Dynamic Steps for Connecting with Nature and Revealing Your Authentic Self,* (Changing Lives Press/Never Sink Books, 2013).
18. Harriet Lerner, Ph.D. *The Dance of Anger: A Woman's Guide to Changing the Patterns of Intimate Relationships,* (New York, NY: Harper Perennial, a division of HarperCollins Publishers, 1985) pages 20-23.
19. Bernie Siegel, M.D., *Love, Medicine & Miracles: Lessons learned about self-healing from a surgeon's experience with exceptional patients,* (New York, NY: Harper & Row, Publishers, Inc., 1986) page 80.
20. Bernie Siegel, M.D., *Love, Medicine & Miracles: Lessons learned about self-healing from a surgeon's experience with exceptional patients,* (New York, NY: Harper & Row, Publishers, Inc.,1986) page 76.

NOTES

21. Susan Campbell, Ph.D., *Getting Real: 10 truth skills you need to live an authentic life,* (An HJ Kramer Book, published in a joint venture with New World Library, 2001) page 202.
22. Susan Campbell, Ph.D., *Getting Real: 10 truth skills you need to live an authentic life,* (An HJ Kramer Book, published in a joint venture with New World Library, 2001) page 203.
23. Eckhart Tolle, *The Power of Now: A Guide to Spiritual Enlightenment,* (Namaste Publishing (1997).
24. David Servan-Schreiber, M.D., Ph.D., *Anticancer: A new way of life,* (New York, NY: Viking Penguin, a member of Penguin Group(USA) Inc., 2008) page 171.
25. Arianna Huffington, *On Becoming Fearless ... in love, work, and life,* (New York, NY: Little, Brown & Company, 2006) page 228.
26. Jaya Chalika and Edward Le Joly, *The Joy of Loving: A guide to daily living with Mother Teresa,* (New York, NY: Penguin Compass, a division of the Penguin Group, 1996), page 33.
27. Sarah Young, *Jesus Calling: Enjoying peace in His presence,* (Nashville, TN: Thomas Nelson, 2004), page XIII.
28. Unity - A positive path for spiritual living, http://content.unity.org/aboutunity/whatwebelieve, (accessed June 10, 2013).
29. Susan M. Love, M.D., & Karen Lindsey, *Dr. Susan Love's Breast Book,* (Cambridge, MA: Da Capo Press, A Member of the Perseus Book Group, 2005), page 471.
30. Wendy Schlessel Harpham, M.D., *Happiness in a Storm,* (New York, NY: W.W. Norton & Company, Inc. 2005), pages 30-31.

TRANSFORMATION

31. Wendy Schlessel Harpham, M.D., *Happiness in a Storm*, (New York, NY: W.W. Norton & Company, Inc. 2005), page 31.

Printed in Great Britain
by Amazon.co.uk, Ltd.,
Marston Gate.